One 2 ONE

One 2 One
© 2000 by Abingdon Press

Printed in the United States of America.

 This book is printed on recycled, acid-free paper.

Cover Art: Mark James

Cover Design: Diana Maio

Abingdon Press

00 01 02 03 04 05 06 07 08 09—10 9 8 7 6 5 4 3 2 1

One 2 ONE

50 Personal Devotions

for Youth Camps,

Retreats, & Trips

The Authors

The authors are all a part of The Edge Ministries. Although we are based in Tennessee now, we want to pay tribute to the people in the places that have shaped us. So with our names, we've included our home states.

Ike Blanton
Florida

Matthew Charlton
Tennessee

Sally Chambers
Ohio

Lief Dove
Texas

Steve Doyal
Tennessee

Duke Gatsos
Ohio

Amanda Goins
Tennessee

Paul Harcey
Minnesota

Darren Hock
New Jersey

Sharri Larson
Minnesota

Trish Pulley
Tennessee

Melissa Roma
Virginia

Mary Schulze
Minnesota

Brad Smith
Tennessee

John Stevens
Tennessee

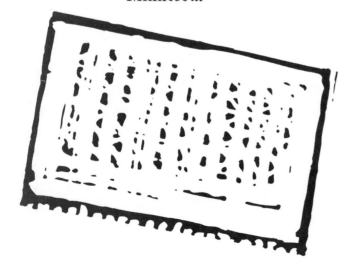

Contents

One 2 ONE

One2One: THE Book

Greetings From the EDGE

We believe that each person is called to have a relationship with God. We want to see youth and adults connecting with the power of God. We believe that spending personal time with God is essential to Christian living, but learning to listen to and talk with God is not so easy. *One2One* is designed to help build the relationship, to make the connection easier.

What Is a One2One?

Put simply, a One2One is a photocopiable, ready-to-go personal devotion. Each devotion begins with Scripture and ends with prayer. In the body is a story with a learning point. Some of the stories come from real-life experiences of an author; others center on a Bible passage. A look through the theme index will show that the stories deal with friendship, trust, teamwork, faith, perseverance, and more.

How Are the Devotions Used?

The devotions in *One2One* were created to make personal devotions easy to plan for group outings. When you plan your retreats, lock-ins, or trips, decide what time you will set aside for personal devotions. Then select the devotions that fit with your trip, photocopy the One2Ones, and bring them along. At devotion time, give each person a Bible and a copy of the One2One. Let each person find a place to be alone for 15 to 30 minutes.

We have developed these devotions to use as personal youth devotions on retreats, but we have found that One2Ones are useful in other ways as well. Here are a few of the many ways that you can use One2Ones:

1. Youth and youth workers can use a One2One in storytelling. The stories make great group devotions or teaching illustrations.

2. Some One2Ones can be converted into skits. Whether you read a story aloud while group members act it out or you create a drama out of the story, there is plenty of room for creativity.

3. Although the devotions are created with outings in mind, these devotions can be used at any time. Leave a copy of the book in a youth room, a school lobby (ask permission), or an office as a way for people to spend some time with God even if they have only a few minutes.

4. Although we have developed these devotions with youth in mind, One2Ones can be used with adults and children as well. The devotions are generally straightforward and easy to draw conclusions from. More mature Christians may want to use the Scripture references for further investigation and meditation.

Where Did the Idea Originate?

The idea for this book originated with the origin of The EDGE Ministries. When The EDGE started leading retreats in 1993, we wanted to be different. We wanted to provide a service to youth groups that no other group was doing. We started an adventure-based ministry that travels to groups to provide program staff. We specialize in team and community building, rock climbing, rappelling, camping, hiking, backpacking, and caving. We can plan and carry out entire retreats, or we can fit into a group's existing schedule.

Since 1993 we have developed some great retreats. Some of those retreats are outlined in our first book, *Retreats From the EDGE.* Through group discussion, we help groups discover the truths about daily spiritual living. We also tie those topics into our group worship.

And all of those retreats call for times of personal devotion—times we call One2One.

Whether The EDGE is working with a group for a day, a weekend, or an extended time, we strive to set up an environment in which growth can take place. We tie all of the events, activities, and spiritual times together. This helps bring into focus the time we spend together. We hope that participants will start to learn that God is part of everything that we do. We hope that groups will recognize the importance of spending alone time, building a relationship with God. We believe One2One will be an exciting tool for you and your group.

Thanks for taking your group to The EDGE. God bless you, and may you have all the best in your ministry.

—Paul Harcey

Permissions and Submissions

We are giving you permission to copy each page for use with your group.

If you have a story of your own for *One2One,* we'd love to see it. Your submission might make it into the next book. Send your story to Paul Harcey at The EDGE Ministries.

The EDGE Ministries
P.O. Box 850
Antioch, TN 37013

E-mail: edge3343@aol.com

ALL TOO *Strange*

Esther 4:9-5:2

Daniel 6:10-12, 16-23

Joshua 1:9

T his story starts out at Camp McCall in South Carolina. I had chosen the Advanced Adventure Recreation track with a group called Outdoor Leadership Lab. When I began the week-long training, I was doing something I had never done before. I had gone with my church youth group to camp, but I had never gone alone. I had to drive six hours to a camp where I knew nobody. To add to the mystery for me, this was a Baptist event, and I had grown up in the Methodist church.

I wasn't crazy about making this trip. I have never done well in new settings, and I have a hard time getting to know new people.

Some people flourish in new places. My friend Megan is one of those people. She is someone who does great in any situation. She is strong in the Spirit and has a great faith. If you meet her and get to know her, you do not forget her. That's Megan—not me. I can go to a camp with 120 people and feel alone.

But at Camp McCall, I soon found out that I wasn't alone. One day during the week, a few of us started talking about the book *Holy Sweat*. The book, about taking risks, was written by Tim Hansel, who works with an organization called Summit Adventures in California. Hal, one of the guys in this conversation, had taken a course at Summit Adventures. My friend Megan worked for a summer at Summit Adventures. So as it turned out, Hal knew Megan. Unreal!

Megan is from Georgia. Hal is from Alabama. I grew up in Minnesota and met Megan in Tennessee. Hal and Megan met in

California. I met Hal in South Carolina. As if that weren't enough, another guy, Charlie, joined our conversation, asking who we were talking about. As it turned out, Charlie and Megan grew up near each other. In fact, Megan's dad was Charlie's doctor. What a small world!

I often remember that week at Camp McCall when working with EDGE Ministries. We ask the youth to take a step out, to push themselves, to move past the edge. When God calls us to go into new territory, God takes us to the edge.

The edge is that unfamiliar place in each of us that gives us a strange feeling in our stomach. The edge can be uncomfortable. The edge forces us to adapt and overcome, to cope and survive. The edge also gives us the opportunity for learning. Every time we stretch out and do something out of the norm, we learn. New experiences help us grow.

The Bible tells about many people who feel alone when God sends them forth to the edge. And God always goes with them. Genesis tells the story of Joseph, whose brothers sell him into slavery in Egypt. Joseph may feel alone, but God is with him in Egypt. In fact, Egypt becomes his home and later becomes the home of his family. Daniel stands alone and praying to God. The king throws him in the lion's den for worshiping God. But Daniel is not alone—God is with him. Queen Esther goes before the king, trembling with the possibility of death. She walks in alone, hoping to save her people. And God is with her.

Something happens when we step out. I ended having a fun trip. I learned a lot. I met God at this camp. Now camp McCall feels like home. I go back each year to see friends.

—Paul Harcey

Prayer: God, take me to the edge. Give me a challenge that only You can get me through. Thank you for your promise to always be with me. In Jesus' name, amen.

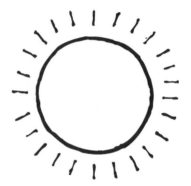

One 2 ONE

ALLELUIA FROM *Head to Toe*

> Psalm 8
> Psalm 19: 1 - 6
> Luke 24:1 - 12

I was at Easter Service at the beautiful Episcopal Cathedral in downtown Chicago. Nothing seemed out of the ordinary for Easter: bells, smells, the bishop, packed pews plus a few extra chairs. And I even had a dress on.

Bishop: "Alleluia, Christ is risen."

Response: "The Lord is risen indeed, Alleluia."

Bishop: "Stop! Let's try that again, with hearts that sing those alleluias and know that Christ is alive."

Wait a second, I thought to myself. *Did the Bishop just stop the Easter service? What kind of church is this?* I was still processing the scene when the deacon came forth to read the Gospel. He was so radiant and full of joy that he appeared to be skipping while holding the Bible in his hands.

At this point I was already filled with that joy, that awe at this day, at this worship. But it didn't stop there. The bishop stepped up to the pulpit to preach. He said, "Be an alleluia from head to toe."

As I sat eagerly soaking in the presence of the risen, living Christ, the bishop walked around the cathedral, sprinkling everyone with water. As he did this, we professed our baptismal vows, renewing the life that knowing Jesus brings.

I have loved Easter ever since I was a little girl. I have always found something innately bright and full of life on that day. But it wasn't the Easter basket loaded with chocolate or the new dress and shoes that hooked me. Somehow the sun always seems to be shining on Easter.

In high school, I found myself arriving home from one service on Easter and turning right around and going back for the next one, just so I could sing those hymns again, hear the trumpets blare and feel that sensation inside once more. Something is different Easter day—we know that our God is alive.

That day in Chicago only enhanced my love for Easter. The bishop made me realize something else as well: Easter isn't just one day. The challenge each day is to remember the living Christ by "being an alleluia from head to toe." How do we do this?

The psalmist writes songs of how the trees, the sky, the sea, the stars, and all of

Creation shouts, "Alleluia!" They become an alleluia by simply being what God created them to be, by being a tree that provides shelter; by being a star that lights the darkness, or by being a stream that carries water to a thirsty world. By being what God created them to be, by answering God's call, they embody alleluias.

So we too can be an alleluia by being ourselves. We can embody alleluias by merely answering God's call for his creation. Through our ears: hearing our God whisper our name and call out to us. Through our eyes: seeing God in everything, seeing beyond the surface, seeing more to this life—the life abundant that Jesus promises. Through our hands: reaching out and receiving from God and then touching the world with God's heart. Through our feet: walking in Jesus' footsteps, taking action, following the call. And through our hearts: knowing Jesus—his joy, his peace, his love, his life. The heart is where alleluias take form, where our alleluias well up and become a part of who we are.

—Sally Chambers

Prayer: Creative God, you created me as a unique being. Show me how I can sing alleluia to you from head to toe. In Jesus' name, amen.

One 2 ONE

ARE YOU Hungry?

Luke 22:8

Romans 8:26-27

Have you noticed that many important events for the early Christians happened around mealtime? Even Jesus performs his first recorded miracle at a wedding banquet. And his last days center on the Passover meal. With each mention of food, there is usually a mention of prayer.

Prayer and food have a lot in common. Eating is how we keep our bodies functioning and alive. We use the nutrition we gain from food for energy, growth, and renewal. Food fills and sustains us but not

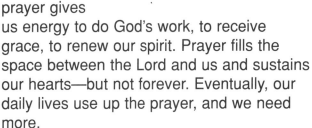

forever. Eventually, our bodies consume the food; and we need more. We must have a continuous supply, or we will get hungry. Likewise, prayer gives us energy to do God's work, to receive grace, to renew our spirit. Prayer fills the space between the Lord and us and sustains our hearts—but not forever. Eventually, our daily lives use up the prayer, and we need more.

One 2 ONE

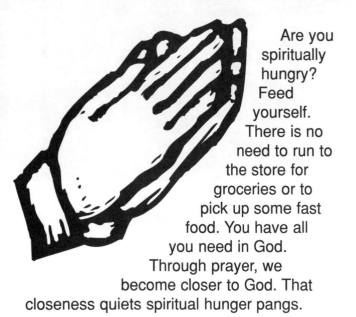

Are you spiritually hungry? Feed yourself. There is no need to run to the store for groceries or to pick up some fast food. You have all you need in God. Through prayer, we become closer to God. That closeness quiets spiritual hunger pangs.

But don't worry—you can't overpray or put on too many extra prayer pounds. Prayer cannot be measured on any scale. But prayer will show up in your relationship with God. It will show up in the strength and boldness that you have for the Lord. Prayer will have an impact on your life and the lives of the ones around you.

—Leif Dove

Prayer: Compassionate God, I want to feel Your closeness. I have fears and worries to tell you about. I also have dreams and thanks to offer you. Thank you for being the Bread of Life that feeds me every day. In Jesus' name, amen.

One 2 ONE

ASK AND YOU SHALL *Receive*

Matthew 7:7-8

There is no Santa Claus. The Tooth Fairy is really your Mom. The Easter Bunny doesn't hide Easter baskets. These statements are all true, reversing the myths I believed as a young child. So if none of those myths is true, what is truth? The truth is an elusive thing.

Discovering truth takes work and research. It takes using your brain and sometimes your body. The ultimate weapon against lies may be asking a good question.

Jesus was The King of the question. He was magnificent at nailing down the truth with key questions. Check out these questions from the book of Matthew:

* If salt loses its saltiness, how can it be made salty again?
* If you greet only your brothers, what are you doing more than others?
* Is life not more important than food, and is the body not more important than clothes?
* Who of you by worrying can add a single hour to his or her life?
* Why do you look at the speck of sawdust in your brother's eye and pay no attention to the plank in your own eye?

One 2 One

* Which of you, if your son asks for bread, will give him a stone?
* Which is easier to say, "Your sins are forgiven," or "Pick up your mat and walk!"?
* Do you believe that I am able to do this?
* Who do you say that I am?
* What good will it be for a man if he gains the whole world, yet forfeits his soul?
* Shouldn't you have had mercy on your fellow servant just as I had on you?
* What do you want me to do for you?
* Which of the two did what his father wanted?
* Whose portrait is (on this coin)? And whose inscription?
* My God, my God, why have you forsaken me?

Jesus often followed up these questions by telling some of the great truths of God and human nature. Jesus knew that the instant of learning often occurs when a question is asked.

We can be like Jesus; we can become truth seekers. The next time you are unsure of something or your information seems a little foggy, clear the air with a question. At times it may be hard, but isn't knowing the truth worth it?

Is Jesus really the Son of God and alive today, or is he just a myth? How do you know? How do you know that Jesus loves you? I know that Jesus is real, alive, and loves me unconditionally and passionately. Ask all the questions to get to the heart of the truth. In the words of Jesus, "What do you think?"

—Duke Gatsos

Prayer: God of Truth, thank you that we can ask any question of you and get the truth. Direct our search, and give us the courage to truly seek. Thank you for walking with us as a guide. In Jesus' name, amen.

One 2 ONE

ASK ANY Cabbage

Job 1:12-22
1 Corinthians 3:1-3
Ephesians 2:1-10

Cabbages don't have much of a life. They grow up to be big, fluffy plants. Then someone comes along and pulls them right out of the ground and cuts them up to make such things as sauerkraut, egg rolls, or the ever-popular cabbage soup. Some cabbages are used in the landscape of houses and office buildings. They make rather nice splashes of color; and if the landscaper gets hungry, there is a tasty cabbage just waiting to become lunch.

Cabbages exist to be consumed. The plants have a bare existence—grown and cultivated to become an appetizer or even a main course.

What would a cabbage say if it could be interviewed? Perhaps it would say: "Well, I sure wish that I could see the Grand Canyon"; or it might ask: "What do mushrooms taste like?"

Humans have it better than cabbages. Most of us are blessed to have people around us who care about us. Many of us have great comforts: air conditioning, cars, CD players, fast food, huge department stores, airplanes, Internet, computers, education, movies, the mall, nice clothes, freedoms of all kinds, comfy houses, refrigerators, interstate highways, church buildings.

It hardly seems possible to have a bare existence within the midst of our prosperity. But sometimes we feel as if we have nothing. Often what is lacking in people's lives is faith. Often we lack faith in friends and family, faith in ourselves, and faith in God.

Many folks may not know how to find this faith. Where do you look? The church, friends, neighbors, relatives will all give you different suggestions. True faith comes from trusting Jesus Christ and living to follow him. This will begin to fill the void and replace all that is wrong with all that is good.

Let's not live like cabbages, which are consumed by the world we live in. With faith, we can step out to the boundaries of life and examine what is beyond.

You can choose to live within a shell of isolation, but you will never experience the fulfilling life that is waiting for you, a life created by God especially for you.

—Matthew W. Charlton

Prayer: Gracious God, forgive me my sins. Let Christ live in me so that I might become alive. Amen.

One 2 ONE

ATTENTION *Shoppers* WAL-MART

Matthew 8:5-13

Mark 8:1-10

Luke 5:12-16

I love Wal-Mart. A person can go at any time and get just about anything. How many times have you gone to Wal-Mart for a pack of batteries and ended up buying motor oil, a picture frame, tie-dye, a bottle of Coke, and some beach towels?

What I like most about Wal-Mart is the commitment to customer service. The essence of customer service is putting the customer needs first. Good customer service is incorporated well within our faith. Take this Wal-Mart example:

Let's say that you are a customer who walks into a store, wanting to buy fishing lures and doilies. You approach a sales associate who is trying to put several cases of stock on a shelf. It is apparent that he doesn't want to help you. He makes eye contact and then quickly looks away. So now you feel as if you're intruding.

You ask him where the lures are, and he

sighs and grunts. He reluctantly points down the aisle and goes back to his business. You buy your lures, walk out, and never come back. This sales associate could have taken 45 seconds to put his stock down, greeted you with a smile, and walked you to the rack of lures. There's no question that he would finish his stocking project on time. Instead, you are turned off, and he is still stressed out. You both lose.

To make a difference in the world, we can simply practice some customer service. We sometimes have the idea that doing an act of kindness requires some big sacrifice on our part. The truth of the matter is that customer service often requires little effort and sacrifice.

We don't have to be a Bible beater or a preacher. We don't have to meet some minimal requirements or pass a personality test. We don't have to give all our money away. We don't have to build houses for Habitat for Humanity, travel to Antigua, or work in a different neighborhood. We don't have to solve the world's problems.

We can simply ask somebody how his or her day was before telling about ours. We can empathize with someone who is going through a hard time. We can take somebody out to lunch. We can congratulate somebody on a job well done. We can tell somebody that we appreciate everything that he or she has done for us. We can pay someone a compliment. We can call a stranger by his or her first name. We can let somebody into the turning lane in front of us. We could be customer service representatives for God.

Jesus practiced this kind of customer service. He healed the sick, made the blind to see, fed thousands, turned water into wine, made the winds subside. To Jesus, these were simple acts. To us, they were miracles.

When we do simple acts, they can seem to other people to be miraculous acts as well. All it takes is an attitude of being God's customer representative. Spend your life trying to get other people to ask you, "Why are you like that?" "Why do you do the things you do?" or "Where do you get your energy." Christians know that that energy comes from God. What can you do today to get someone to wonder what makes you tick?

—Darren Hoch

Prayer: God, You treat us better than we deserve. Give us the wisdom, courage, and compassion to treat others as you treat us. In Jesus Christ's name, amen.

One 2 ONE

BURNT CARDBOARD *Casserole*

> Matthew 7: 13-14
>
> Matthew 5: 1-16

My mother is an excellent cook. I remember eating some fabulous meals when I was growing up. Baked chicken, scalloped potatoes, mac and cheese, fresh green beans and corn. Yum!

This excellent cooking, however, has not always been the case. Apparently, there have been some doozies of dishes out there in the distant past. My father has told me about at least two incidences from the early years, regarding some questionable food products that my mother concocted.

There was a meatloaf many years ago that had basketball-like qualities. That is, it bounced. I would like to think that at least Mom tried. However, I am grateful that my solid-food diet consisted of strained peas at the time.

But the meatloaf was not Mom's worst meal. She received a new recipe for a casserole, calling for rice and pimentos. Rice, as you may know, is usually easy to make. The problem was that Mom used Minute Rice® instead of the long-grain, longer-cooking rice. Minute Rice® cooks in minutes and is not suited for dishes that need to be baked for an hour.

My father told me that the casserole tasted slightly worse than burnt cardboard. The pimentos floated placidly in grease above the burnt, ricey residue. Mom was horrified, and Dad was stunned. Our dog even rejected this creation.

What's the point? First, pay attention to the rice you are using. Second, don't cook the wrong thing too long.

Many people are feeding their spiritual lives with Minute Rice® when they need long-grain. Your Christian walk needs constant sustenance. Christians are called to community worship, to service and missions, to love of God and neighbor.

Are you getting all you can when you worship alone? No, you are not. Are you experiencing all you can out of your Christian life when you choose to always play and never serve? No, you are not. Can you fully experience the love of God without loving your neighbor? No, you cannot.

To feed your soul, do not neglect the ingredients of your Christian life simply because you have a recipe. Make sure that you use the right stuff. If you start with the wrong stuff and keep cooking it, you will burn out, lose faith quickly, and become as tasteless as burnt cardboard. But with the right stuff destined for the long term, your life can be a gourmet meal.

—Matthew W. Charlton

Prayer: Creator God, you provide for us all that we need for salvation, faith in Christ Jesus as savior. Help me to walk in Christ's way. Amen.

One 2 ONE

CALLING ALL Abrahams

Hebrews 11:8-11
James 2:20-26

I'd like to talk with some of the Old Testament heroes. I really wish I knew some of them. Wouldn't it be cool to be able to talk to Abraham when a family member gets cancer? He would surely have some good advice.

But the great men and women of the Old Testament are nothing out of the ordinary. In fact, there is only one simple quality they exhibit that sets them apart. It is this quality that allows God to use them in extraordinary ways. These big-time heroes trust God and act. It's that simple.

Noah stands up to criticism while he is building the ark. David smashes Goliath despite the odds against him. Esther stands up and saves her people in the face of certain death. To me, however, Abraham is the prototype of the man of faith. God asks him to leave his old way of life and move to the Promised Land. Abraham drops everything in the sand and goes. No questions, no grumblings, no back talk, no "God, you have got to be kidding me!" Abraham just moves.

I wonder what objections we would make today. "God, what about the car? What about the garage I keep it in? And what about the house I live in? God, my daughter is too

young to move; she will never make it. God, my wife was going to go back to school. What about my career; I was just promoted. What? No TV, no video games, no music videos?"

Can you hear the argument? Have you been making the same argument? Does today's Abraham have any more to lose than the original? No, of course not. What Abraham realized was that God was in control. God would provide for Abraham wherever he went and would give what he needed. That has never changed—God will provide.

Another Abraham could be out there. In fact, one could be reading this paper right now. It could be you. All you need to do is what Abraham did: Trust in God and act. When you act as Abraham did, God will give you more than what you started with.

—Duke Gatsos

Prayer: Loving God, we have lots of reasons for not trusting you. Help us to remember that we can follow where you lead without fear. Thank you for walking with us. In Jesus' name, amen.

One 2 ONE

CATCH THE *Wave*

Romans 8:9-11
Galatians 5:16, 25

Surfing may look like an easy, care-free sport. After all, surfers seem so easy-going. But let me be one of the first to tell you that surfing is by no means easy. Growing up near the beach in Florida, I struggled with surfing for many years. I eventually got to be okay, but I never really developed great skill at it. Surfing didn't engulf my life, and that lack of devotion showed whenever I hit the beach.

One of my favorite things about surfing was the fact that I could control the wave—or at least I felt as if I could. I felt as if the wave was there for my bidding when and where I needed it to go. I was the one who chose which tube to enter, which wave to catch, and what I would do while on the wave. It seemed to get a lot easier at that point. I was in complete control, with the salt water slapping my face and the sun beating my back. I was lording over nature.

My confidence came to an abrupt stop one day. I saw a wave slightly larger than I was used to. It provided ample space to maneuver, so I was enjoying the ride. That's when I crashed and burned. I "busted hard" off the wave and hit the ocean floor, scraping my face against the sand. I came up under my board, and one of the fins did a very nice slice-and-dice number on my shoulder (I still have the scar). After this experience, I reveled in the power and majesty of nature and of the waves slamming into the shoreline. I ran to my car

Permission to photocopy this page is granted to the purchaser of *One 2 One*.
© 2000 by Abingdon Press.

and dressed my superficial wounds, which were not nearly as painful as my trampled pride. When I went back out to the beach, I lay down on the towel gazing at the water. That's when an older guy came up and started talking to me.

"Hey, saw ya bust out there. You OK?"

I responded with a not-so-considerate, "Yeah," hoping that he would take a hint and leave me in peace. He didn't. He continued to talk and evaluate my surfing style.

I was ready to tune him out, then he said something that really hit home. "You know, you can be a good surfer when you control the wave. But the only way to be a *great* surfer is to *let the wave control you*."

What he said has stuck with me. It makes sense not only for surfing but also for my Christian life. When I control what I do, I can be a good Christian. But when I let the Holy Spirit control me, I will be a great Christian. Sometimes I still bust, but I now have a lot more fun.

—Ike Blanton

Prayer: Thank you, God, for the way you gently live within me: leading, teaching, overcoming, and comforting. Thank you for letting me ride the wave with you. In Jesus' name, amen.

 One 2 ONE

COME TO Me

Matthew 11:28-30
Psalm 121

The youth I know are busy. My friends are in demand before and after school and in the evenings, and then they are expected to finish homework, be good friends, and be responsible in their families. Planning youth group events is not easy, because I can't find the youth. They're too busy.

Jesus has help for us. Jesus says, "Come to me, all you that are weary and are carrying heavy burdens [*I know about them*] and I will give you rest. Take my yoke upon you, and learn from me." This passage is most interesting in what it doesn't say. Jesus doesn't tell us that he will take away the burdens. He doesn't even exactly tell us that he will help us.

He does tell us to replace our burdens with his yoke, which is a tool to help carry heavy loads. We know that the yoke doesn't take away the burden, but it takes away the weight of the burden by sharing it. So Christ isn't promising to take the burden away but to share it. We can put aside what is weighing down our hearts and work with Christ.

Christ does not tell us that things will be easy. If that were the case, he would tell us to forget the yoke. He would say that there really is no burden. Of course, there are burdens; but when they are carried with Christ's yoke, we are freed from the weight of those burdens.

Christ calls the tired, the busy, and the stressed. He consoles and relieves our weariness. What a great promise! It's the best prayer that I can think of for busy people. Listen to Christ's words. Go to Christ. Ease your burdens and walk alongside Christ.

—Sharri Larson

Prayer: Caring God, I need the lighter burden that you promise. Give me rest from weariness and stress. Thank you for your love. In Jesus' name, amen.

One 2 ONE

CREATED IN God's Image

> Genesis 1:26-31
> 1 Timothy 4:4-5

I'd like to introduce you to Tara. You probably already know someone just like her. She is of average height and average weight, and she looks rather ordinary. She doesn't wear designer clothes. She doesn't fix her hair or wear make-up. She doesn't hang out with the popular crowd. In fact, she has only a few close friends.

Like many girls her age, she has dreams of dating the captain of the basketball team, going to the prom, having a successful career after college. But even though she has all of those great dreams for herself,

Tara doesn't believe that they will come true. Her dreams require things that she doesn't see in herself: beauty, charisma, and intelligence. These are the things she thinks that she needs.

At the age of 15, she looks at the world around her and feels inadequate. Magazines, movies, television, and peers all tell her that she should wear certain clothes, have her hair cut "just right," be a certain height and a certain weight. Add to the pressure to look a certain way the demands to get good grades and to go on to a prestigious college so that she can have that career. Tara not only has to be beautiful, but she also has to be "successful." By this yardstick, most of us wouldn't measure up.

She feels as if she is not good enough, not pretty enough, not smart enough. Of course, she is wrong. Tara is created by God in God's image. Paul tells Timothy: "Everything created by God is good, and nothing is to be rejected, provided it is received with thanksgiving; for it is sanctified by God's word and by prayer" (1Timothy 4:4-5).

That means that Tara is valuable, since she is created by God. So am I. So are you. There is nothing average or ordinary about you. God knew you before you were born and created you exactly as you should be. And that makes you beautiful.

Do you know someone who feels the way Tara does? How can you serve him or her? What do you do when you feel like Tara?

Take a look around at God's beautiful creation; then look in the mirror and look again at God's beautiful creation.

—Mary Shultze

Prayer: Compassionate God, thank you for your deep love for me and for everyone around me. Help me show other people the love you have for them. In Jesus' name, amen.

One 2 ONE

Do THE RIGHT *Thing*

Luke 16:10
Galatians 6:9-10

Is it wrong to cheat? Is it wrong to steal? Most people would say that it is. From our parents and teachers we learn that honesty is important. Sometimes, though, the questions can be a little more difficult to answer:

- ❁ Is it wrong to copy a friend's worksheet right before class because you forgot to do the assignment?
- ❁ When the fast-food server forgets to charge me for the extra soda and the side order of fries, is it wrong not to tell him or her?
- ❁ Is it wrong to sneak into my mom's purse and "borrow" $10, intending to pay her back only if she notices and asks me about it?

But sometimes we justify our actions:

- ❁ If I don't copy the worksheet, I'll get a zero, which will bring my grade down. It's not as if I couldn't have done the worksheet myself, so I'll get the grade I would have gotten if I had done the assignment.
- ❁ The fast-food server made the mistake, so it's not my fault. Besides, it would take too long to redo the whole bill if I told; and it's only a couple dollars.
- ❁ Mom probably won't even notice. But if she does, I'll pay her back. She should be giving me more allowance, anyway, because I do a lot of work around the house.

What difference do these decisions make? It's not as if we're killing someone or doing something else that's really bad. But as Christians, we need to take every action seriously. God would not stop loving us if we copied a worksheet or cheated on a test, but we are still called to do what is right. In the Bible, it is called being righteous.

Doing the right thing in all situations is probably impossible. But often we know what is right and we have the opportunity to clearly choose whether to do right or wrong. Often the *doing* can be hard. It takes honesty, honesty about our motives and our selfishness. It requires strength and humility. When we do what's right, we don't always get instant rewards.

Doing what's right is not always easy. Following Christ can be hard, and swallowing our pride can be difficult. But if there is one way in which we can truly live our faith, it's to do what's right even in seemingly unimportant, smaller situations. In Matthew, Jesus tells us that when we are faithful in small things, we will gain the strength to be faithful in large things. Consider it good practice to do what's right from day to day; for God has many challenges ahead, when you will solve even greater problems.

Paul gives the Galatians clear advice: "Let us not grow weary in doing what is right, for we will reap at harvest-time, if we do not give up. So then, whenever we have an opportunity, let us work for the good of all, and especially for those of the family of faith."

—Sharri Larson

Prayer: Thank you for the good news: You promise to always be with us, to guide us, and to give us strength, even when it's hard to do the right thing. In Jesus' name, amen.

One 2 ONE

DROP THE Flashing Sign

> Jeremiah 29:13
> John 10:10
> Psalm 8:148

Why haven't I had one of those earth-moving, bang-boom experiences with God?" a junior high friend of mine wanted to know. She was continually looking for an experience where God knocked her flat on her face with "warm-fuzzy" emotion.

Because she didn't get the experience by her senior year of high school, she has now given up on God.

I know other teens who are content to accept a God who doesn't do much of anything. They believe in God without a doubt. They're regular church attendees but really don't think that God is active anymore. They believe in God in Heaven, they just don't see God on Earth.

Both sides miss something—they miss God. Neither truly experiences God fully. Neither truly experiences this life. One is stuck on seeking the extraordinary experience; the other is stuck on experiencing nothing more than surface-level ordinary.

The clear experience of God is found in the ordinary, everyday things. There's no need to doubt the awesomeness of those intense, lightening-bolt God moments, but relying on them in order to believe in God is like missing most of a movie.

A young college student from Vietnam had grown up with a mixture of Christian and Buddhist teachings. One day he said to a Christian friend, "What I don't understand is the 'faith' part. I can get the rest, but please explain to me what faith is."

One 2 ONE

Permission to photocopy this page is granted to the purchaser of *One 2 One*.
© 2000 by Abingdon Press.

33

The stunned friend asked him, "Are the stars out tonight?"

He said, "No. It's cloudy and dark."

The friend looked him in the eyes and said, "Ah, but you know that the stars are still there."

He nodded slowly and whispered, "Now I get it."

The next day he tromped into the friend's dorm room after class; plopped onto the bed; and, with a pouting smirk on his face said, "You know, life was so ordinary before. I was walking to class, and I saw a tree; but I didn't see just a tree. I saw a tree that God had created, that was amazingly designed. I saw a tree that somehow, in its very essence, seemed to tell of its Maker."

Then as a smile stretched across his face, he added sarcastically, "Now nothing will be the same. Thank you very much!"

Take the experience of God and add it to the everyday, taken-for-granted flowerpot of life; and the ordinary becomes extraordinary.

The Scriptures tell us over and over again that we will find God where we seek God. If we seek God only in Heaven, we won't find God on earth. If we seek God only in the intense, dramatic turnarounds, we will miss experiences of God. But if we seek God in the moment-to-moment loves and pains of life with all our heart, then we will experience God more fully.

Are you waiting for bolts from the sky? Or are you allowing our God and Savior to be a part of the smallest, most ordinary moment of every day?

—Sally Chambers

Prayer: Dear Lord, may your grace open our eyes to see you more clearly in the tiniest details of our life so that your immeasurable desire to be close to us will come alive. Amen.

One 2 ONE

FACE TO Face

| 1 Corinthians 13:9-13 |

spent an hour and a half driving to her house, and so many questions ran through my head. What color would her eyes be? Would she be taller than I am? I knew that she was younger than I am, would she look a lot younger? Would our meeting be awkward or easy? My mind took me from one extreme to the other and back in that hour and a half. I came to the door and knocked, with a lump in my throat the size of my Adam's apple.

I was a little relieved when I first saw her. From her smile I knew that she was pleased to see me. We both relaxed as we got to know each other. By the stories I have heard, I had great luck on this, my first blind date. I had spoken to this girl on the phone a few times, but I still wondered if she was right for me. No matter how much I tried to deny it, those first moments meeting her face to face were going to be a factor.

Since we have adapted to the computer age, more and more relationships are developed over the modem lines. Internet chat rooms and e-mail addresses have become popular media for communication.

One of my friends once e-mailed me that he felt more comfortable talking about deeper feelings over the modem than in person. I can certainly understand his thinking, because there is so much more risk involved when you are talking to a person face to face. You can see a person's reactions when you are sitting with him or her. Facial expression tells more than our words can convey. Don't you just hate it when your friends know what you're going to say before you say it?

Many of us are intimidated by beautiful people. Others of us are repulsed by people with certain physical characteristics. No matter how great the relationship feels over the phone lines, it becomes more real by meeting face to face. I have heard stories of wonderfully deep relationships created over the Internet that came apart when the two met face to face. True intimacy happens when people bring these cyber relationships into the physical world. That is the world we live in, so we shouldn't try to get around it.

God intends for us to relate to each other face to face. God wants the same type of intimate relationship with us. It is easy to keep God at a distance. We sacrifice certain parts of our lives for God, but others we hold onto. We are afraid to open our lives completely in God's presence. If God gets too close, all of our flaws might show. It is difficult to get past the masks to reveal our true selves to God.

In the same way, we are often afraid to see God in God's perfection. We create images of what God is like. It is impossible to see all of God's wonder and glory. If we see God truly, we worry that we might not like what we see. All of these misconceptions and fears keep us from seeing each other face to face.

However, if we don't struggle to see God face to face, we are missing out on a truly intimate relationship. When we take God seriously, we will be able to look God in the eye and say, "You are perfect, and I want to love you in all your power and might." We can hear God say back, "I accept you just as you are, and I love you unconditionally— even with all of your faults, quirks, and imperfections."

—Duke Gatsos

Prayer: You are perfect, God. I know that I am not perfect, but you still love me. I want to know you. I want to love you in all your power and might. Help me see you and love you. In Jesus' name, amen.

One 2 ONE

FINDING SWEET Water

> James 4:9-10
>
> Matthew 5:8
>
> John 4:10-14

I was taking a backpacking trip in the Boundary Waters Canoe Area (BWCA). This extensive series of lakes that make up the border of Minnesota and Canada is a great place left behind by the last ice age. It is quiet, peaceful, and awesome up there. Anyway you look at the scenery, you can see God.

One of the tricky aspects of the back woods is the water. You can never trust the quality. Our bodies get used to organisms in the water that we drink all the time. When we change our source of water, it can make bad things happen. So the water we encounter in nature must sometimes be treated to make it safe to drink.

If a person is packing light, he or she can bring iodine tablets that will kill everything in the water. The bad part is that the tablets can leave a taste and color in the water. Also, the tablets take about 20 minutes to work. Or if there is time, the water can be boiled to kill the germs. Once the temperature gets up to boiling, the bad stuff is dead.

Both of these methods work and have their place. But I am a gearhead. Everything has its own gear. There is gear for

computers, for bikes, for school, and for work. The gear that I really like is for adventure activities. So here comes the gear. Outdoor equipment companies are now making water filters. These things are great! They are small—not as small as the iodine tablets, but small enough. They filter out all of the bad stuff—not only the bacteria that can be in the water, but viruses and pollution as well.

All of these contaminants can get into a water supply and can hurt the body of the drinker. Some of these contaminants will mess with your body for a short time, some will build up over time to mess up everything in your body, and some can keep coming back to hurt you again and again. So you pour your water through the filter, and you get pure water. Does any of this sound familiar?

We are all like the water in a stream. Many ideas are dumped into us, and we carry them downstream with us. These ideas can be good or bad. They can help us or hurt us. Once we go through the filter, we can be pure. God is our purifier. God pours us out of the polluted stream and filters out all of the bad stuff. That way we can used to help other people. Just as we do not want to take in bad water to drink, God does not want us to hurt others because our hearts and actions are not pure. If we are filled up with all of the crud that this world tries to get us to believe, we are like the polluted water—we just hurt. But if we go through God and are purified, we can be the spring of life for those around us.

That is what God calls us to do. God wants us to be pure of heart. In that way, we can be like a cool glass of clean water for those we encounter. We can be refreshing. We can help sustain life. We can help be what they are looking for, without adding any more pollution to their system.

Seek God out—be purified.

—Paul Harcey

Prayer: Holy God, be my purifier. Pour me out of the polluted streams and filter out the bad stuff. Make me suitable to help and not hurt other people. Be the spring of life that flows through me. In Jesus' name, amen.

One 2 ONE

FOLLOW THE *Leader*

> Matthew 4:18-22
>
> Matthew 8:18-22

Something about Bible Camp turns seemingly regular kids into crazy, spontaneous, surprising people. My summers as a Bible camp counselor allowed me to see God working in campers in so many ways.

One week, my full cabin of eighteen girls was out on a picnic lunch. They quickly finished eating and wanted to play a game of Follow the Leader. We jumped up, and I led them frolicking around the lawn.

I led the group hopping and dancing to the beach front. They followed me as I took off my shoes, and we splashed a bit in the shallow water. I then stepped up onto the dock; and, as craziness overcame me, I ran to the end of the dock and plunged in. The water was over my head. When I rose from the water, I expected to see the girls shocked at my wildness, amazed, and laughing at me for jumping into the water fully dressed.

Instead, I saw every one of their little legs jumping into the cold water after me. They splashed in, rising with shouts of laughter at the sheer fun of something so spontaneous.

I hadn't really expected them to follow me. I expected them to think better and more thoroughly. Why would they want to jump in? The water was cold. The girls were fully dressed. The money, notes, and canteen cards in their pockets were ruined by the

water. Some of the girls didn't have many extra clothes along, because their mothers had carefully counted out their clothes for the week.

But it was most striking that they would follow *me*. If I, as a college-age counselor in the lives of kids for only one week, can encourage them to follow me, how much more can Jesus call us to follow him! And how much more can Jesus affect their lives, bring them the joy and spontaneity of believing!

When eighteen fifth and sixth grade girls plunged into the lake after me, they didn't even think about it. I just jumped. They just followed. It was a simple decision. It reminds me of two equally simple, unquestioned decisions the disciples made about following Jesus. The two passages in Matthew tell about Jesus calling four of the disciples, Simon, Andrew, James, and John.

In both stories, the new-found disciples don't stop to question this stranger, who is calling them to follow. Simon and Andrew drop their nets and leave their jobs in the middle of the workday for a promise that probably didn't even make sense, to follow a person they had never met. James and John leave their father, Zebedee, alone in the boat. What would that have meant to Zebedee? These disciples show an incredible faith.

—Sharri Larson

Prayer: Dear God, grant us the spontaneity, the willingness, the courage, and the desire to follow immediately when Christ calls us.

FOR YOUR EYES Only

Isaiah 6:5

I am a snow chaser. Like those people who follow tornadoes or sports; I follow the snow. I was born and reared in south Texas, and the sight of snow came only through TV or photographs. Since I have moved to Tennessee, I have come to love the snow. I like to find a snowflake as it is coming down, run under it, and try to catch it on my tongue. I can get that cool feeling of the snow on my tongue, the cold changing to wet.

I find the most beautiful patterns, shadows, and textures in snow that my eyes have never seen. I often see such treasures when I am by myself and not even looking for them. Sometimes I seem to be in a trance of purity, subtlety, and harmony. Everything seems to be right in the world and I am just in "the zone."

These wintery sights are worth sharing, so I rush to find friends or family. When I drag them back to see

what I have seen, what was perfect and so right just a moment ago is now melted or new snow has fallen and covered up the masterpiece. So, then I'm frustrated. God had set before me visions from heaven, and I was not able to share them with anyone else. But then I got to thinking about what God is all about. God is about giving us what we need when we need it. God is about building relationships with us so that we can be used to help others along their way. God is about revealing to us in the knee-deep snow just a glimpse, just enough to keep us looking for more.

Would God have showed me such sights without letting me share them with others? Yes and no. My time in the snow could have been the Heavenly Parent playing with me, his child. Although I did not get to share that moment with anyone else, I do get to tell about what I learned from it. God showed something to this nutty person who went out in the knee-deep snow.

One 2 ONE

The message is not the snow itself. The message is how I see the snow.

Others can see God's messages through countless other ways. And, if I really want them to know about the purity, subtly, and harmony, I can show them by how I live. The way I live reflects what God is doing in my life.

God opens our eyes to show us the glory. God does this in many ways: through the Bible, through the actions of other people, in a sunset, or out in the snow. Our responsibility is to show God's glory to others. Show them by your life, by your actions, by telling them how God is working in your life.

God has a unique relationship with each of us. God will treat you in a unique way. If God decides to reveal something to you, treasure that moment and understand that it might be for you alone. Share it with others in the way you live, not by dragging them through the knee-deep snow.

—Leif Dove

Prayer: God, open our eyes to see your glory around us. Thank you for glimpses each day. In Jesus' name, amen.

One 2 ONE

GIVE ME Direction

2 Timothy 3:16,17

With sweaty palms I dialed the 6 digits. I paused before I hit the last one. As my fear mounted, I quickly pushed the clicker on my phone. The dial tone signaled the end of my courage. I had done this three times now.

I gave myself one more chance. I got up some courage and told myself, "No more hanging up. Dial all seven numbers this time!" I cleared my throat and hummed to make sure that my voice sounded confident. *Punching five digits. . . . I can do this. . . . Now 6. . . . Oh, wow! . . . I've done 7! . . . It's ringing!* I recalled the script that I had run over in my head for all day. *Oh, no! Someone's answering. It's a deep voice, probably her dad. Oh, man!*

"Is Amy there?"
"Who's calling?"
"Duke."
"Just a minute."
Teasing her he calls to her, "It's Duuuke."

She whines back, "Daaaad!" Then her sweet voice says, "Hello?"

"Amy, it's Duke."
"Hey!"

I think *Wow, that was encouraging!* I eventually relaxed and remembered the script that I had memorized. We had a great conversation, and we set a date. I hung up and pumped my fist in the air, silently screaming, "Yeah!" Then I thought, *Wait a minute. I don't know how to get to her*

house. I'm going to have to call back again. Ugh!

How embarrassing! After the emotional moment, I needed some facts.

I've seen many people go through miraculous, pumped up, emotionally charged conversions. For the next week after an emotional experience, they talk about Jesus to everybody they see. They can't really explain much about who Jesus is or about or how they know he is real. They don't really know how they became a Christian or why. They "just know." Soon afterward, the emotions die out, and they go back to their old way of life.

While I don't doubt the truth of their conversion, emotions, and desire, I do know that a life-changing commitment to God that sticks requires some knowledge of God's Word. God has spoken it to us for just that reason: to ground our faith on something solid, something everlasting.

Nobody knows the way to God's house, except God. You can ask God to show you how to get there. The Bible gives the directions to a real, relevant-to-life commitment to Jesus. Once anchored on God's Word, the Holy Spirit guides us to make powerful decisions.

The truths of the Scripture come alive to have an impact on our lifestyle. Just give God a call, open the Bible, and ask God how to get home.

—Duke Gatsos

Prayer: God, I'm asking. Show me the way home. Let me rest in you. Let me sit at your feet. In Jesus' name, amen.

One 2 ONE

GRANDMA'S SECRET *Recipe*

> 1 Kings 17:17-24
>
> Romans 8:11
>
> John 15:7

M y grandmother makes the best vegetable soup I have ever tasted. I haven't learned yet how she does it. It's her secret recipe. Unfortunately, there are so many wonderful things going on that are secrets. We tend to protect things that have the most value to us. But the Bible tells us to share the things that are the most valuable to us. So in the interest of full disclosure, I want to tell you about a secret of the faith that I stumbled across the other day.

It was a story of a man bringing another person back to life. While it is certainly not surprising that I would find a story like this in the Bible, I was surprised that I had never heard of it before. I mean, it's a big deal when someone is resurrected from the dead. By no means does God mean for this to be a secret; there are a few good lessons in it, not to mention the recipe for raising someone from the dead.

This story comes from the beginning of the ministry of Elijah, a prophet of God. It is one of many miracles that Elijah performs during his life. God has ordered Elijah to live with a widow and her son. The widow's son becomes ill and dies.

We don't know if it is originally in God's plan for the son to be raised from the dead. There is no mention of God planning a display of power in the situation. There is no prophecy from Elijah about the depth of God's love and mercy. So, why does God raise the son?

The answer is in verse 22: "The LORD listened to the voice of Elijah; the life of the child came into him again, and he revived." What an amazing statement! God resurrected the widow's son because Elijah cried out, asking God to let the boy live. No secrets here.

We have access to the same power that Elijah used. The spirit that raises the dead lives in us. The Bible also says that if we stay joined to Jesus Christ and let his teachings become part of us, we can pray anything and that prayer will be answered.

Don't let the great stories of the children of God be secrets. Get out and tell one today. God wants to tell others of incredible love. That love is enough to raise the dead. And it's no secret.

—Duke Gatsos

Prayer: God we are simple people with desperate needs. Thank you for hearing the cries of your children and responding with love and mercy. Thank you for allowing us to tell the juiciest secret we know: the message of your great love for us.

One 2 ONE

G R O W I N G SPIRITUAL *feet*

O ften the first hole in a sock appears at the big toe. It's an annoying trait of socks that holes eventually appear. We are reminded that it is time to buy a new pair or a whole package of socks whenever there is extensive hole propagation.

What happens to you when you get a hole worn in your spirit? Do you go out and purchase a new spirit? Can you mend it with your sewing kit? Whatever you do, however, the holes continue to appear.

Often we look at external forces that are causing our spirit to get worn down when, perhaps, it might be more beneficial to look at how your own spirit might be causing the holes.

Take a hearty look at your "spiritual feet." Take some time to wiggle your toes in the sand of God's love and Christ's salvation. Make sure that what you stand on will support you and not wear you down.

How does a spirit get worn down? Many parts of our lives drain us when they could be filling us up. Schoolwork could be edifying when often it is boring, busy work. Serving in a position in the church could be uplifting when sometimes it is not. Participating in athletics can help both spirit and body. But

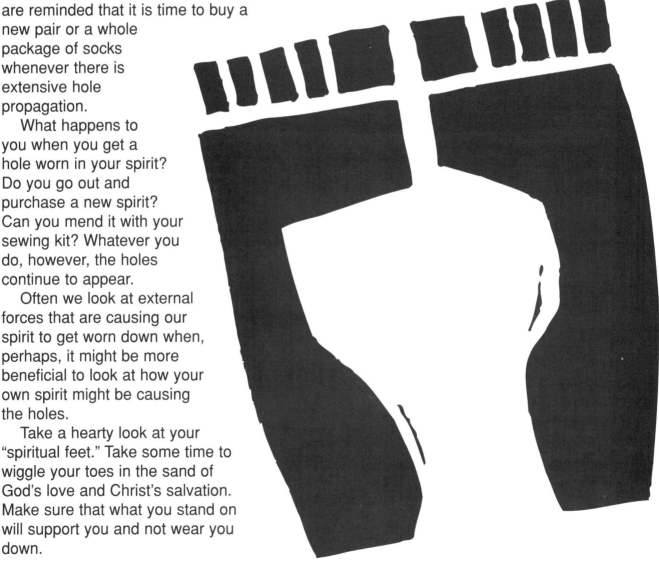

47

often the requirements for sports consume a large portion of time. You may go home, knowing that there are chores to be done. You go to bed, knowing that you have to wake up the next morning just to do it all over again.

Every time you make a commitment, some of your free time is going to vanish. And if you wear many hats, you will end up simply trying to get by.

Stop this madness. It's time to sit down and set your priorities. What is most important? What activities can you do without? What activities are using a lot of time and are not very productive? These activities are wearing holes in your spiritual socks.

You can replace your spiritual socks by doing what is important. You can repair them by losing what is simply time consuming. Remember to walk closely with God. God will make sure that your spiritual socks are always in good repair.

—Matthew W. Charlton

Prayer: God, you know that I am involved in many activities. I am a busy person. Help me to never lose sight of you. And when I stray, give me the strength to return to your open arms. Amen.

One 2 ONE

HOW TO BE Humble

> Micah 6:8
>
> Philippians 2:3-4

I was flipping through my Bible to begin writing a devotion on the parable of the fig tree. Because it's a short parable (it doesn't even have a subtitle in my user-friendly version of the Bible), I was taking a few minutes to find it. During my search, I ran into a bookmark that had some notes scribbled on the back of it. The notes caught my attention, so I stopped looking for the fig tree chapter. The notes said:

"What does the Lord require?"
"What does walking humbly mean?"
and finally,
"Who is someone you know who walks humbly?"

A simple lesson in life was staring right there at me. The lesson is simple to comprehend but not so simple to live out. We often think that God requires an abundance of things from us. Although God would probably like for us to do many things and has given us the guidelines and tools to achieve many things, this passage says that God requires only three things: Do justice, love kindness, walk humbly with your God.

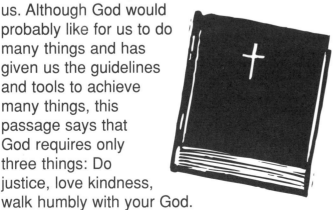

That's it! Okay, maybe that does sound like a lot; but at least we know what to shoot for. Now, what is this about walking humbly? How do we do it? Paul tells the Philippians to "do nothing from selfish ambition or conceit, but in humility regard others as better than yourselves." In order to walk humbly, we can't consider ourselves better than anyone else. In our society, this seems like unusual thinking. We have tests to prove who is smarter, competitions to prove who is faster or stronger, and bank accounts to prove who is wealthier. But humility doesn't depend on where you fall on those lists. Humility is an attitude that considers others first.

And that brings us to the last question: Who is someone you know who walks humbly? Think of someone you know who "walks humbly." Don't just keep reading this. Stop and really think of someone you know who puts others first, who is the cheerleader for everyone, who makes you feel like a worthwhile person. Is this person someone you like to be around? Can you take this role in someone else's life?

Today take the time to build up someone else. Take the time to serve your best friend today. Take the time to serve a stranger. When you do, you will be doing one thing that God requires.

As long as you do this, you have opened the door to allow yourself to love your neighbor as yourself.

—Melissa Roma

Prayer: God help us imitate Jesus Christ, who was truly God but who did not strive to be equal with God. Instead, he gave up everything and became a slave when he became like one of us. Teach us to be that humble. In the name of Jesus Christ, amen.

One 2 ONE

JONAH AND THE Vine

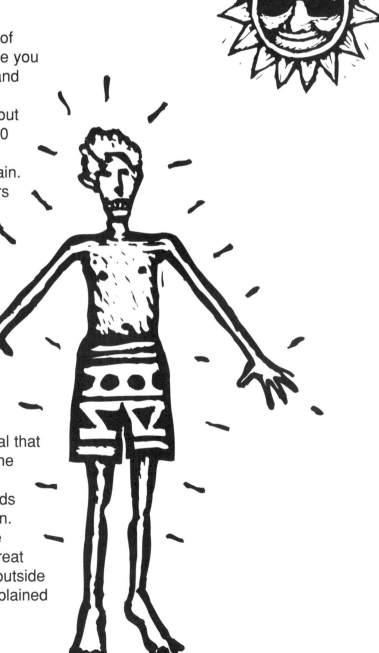

Jonah 4

Maybe you have heard the story of Jonah and the big fish. But have you ever heard the story of Jonah and the vine?

Well, Jonah is just plain tuckered out from the biggest revival ever (120,000 turn to God in Nineveh), and he sits down to rest. And he starts to complain. The sick reality of human nature rears its head when Jonah gets angry with God right after this miraculous conversion of the multitudes.

Once again, God shines love down on Jonah and provides him the shelter of a vine. The vine gives Jonah shade and protection from the world. It seems like some sort of oasis in the desert. Since Jonah hasn't learned from the big fish ordeal that God will provide, God shrivels the vine and Jonah is once again exposed to the elements. The Book of Jonah ends with Jonah getting fried in the hot sun.

When I first read this, I was a little confused. I mean, here's Jonah, a great prophet of the one true God, sitting outside getting skin cancer because he complained about having to preach to Gentiles. I finished Chapter 4 and quickly turned the page, looking for Chapter 5. But to no avail. Why does God leave us with this shriveled vine story?

A little reflection provides an answer. The point of the vine story is that God is more concerned about having a relationship with each of us than for our safety, comfort, or contentedness. The next time you wonder why God hasn't given you everything you want, think about the shriveled vine. Fill your mind with how you can work to help people gain eternal life. That's what God wants.

—Duke Gatsos

Prayer: God, use me to help someone come to know you. Help me put my life in perspective. Fill my mind with following your will and remove my selfish desires. Thank you for giving me the greatest gift I can imagine: eternal life. May I never take it for granted. In Jesus' name, amen.

One 2 ONE

KING OF THE Jungle

John 15:1-11

I never saw any grapes on the vines, but we still called them grapevines. One of my favorite activities as a young boy was swinging on the vines. I was always fortunate to live near a patch of woods where I could indulge this passion. I got quite adept at picking out the good vines. They came up from the ground and wrapped their tentacles around the upper branches of tall trees. We would cut them about four feet up from the ground and then it was time for TARZAN. "Ahhhhhhahhhhahhhahhhhahhhhh" (or whatever that Tarzan yell was).

I remember one time in particular, when some friends and I were on an adventure in the forest. When we played, the forest became our personal jungle. We found a vine that someone else had already cut off for swinging. The tree was so tall, we couldn't even see the top. My buddies and I stood there and surveyed the scene. The path of the vine would swing us over a drop-off. My vine swinging expertise was legendary, so everyone looked at me and I knew that I was going to be the first Tarzan of the day.

I took the rough and shaggy vine in my hands and gave it a tug. It seemed solid, so I flashed a confident smile at my pals. I took several steps back so that I could get a running start. As I was airborne, I had visions of grace and dexterity. I knew that I was king of the jungle. I was ready to let loose a Tarzan yell when I heard the snap. I was traveling the speed of sound and several stories above the earth when I was suddenly in free fall.

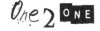

I can still hear the sickening thud my body made as it rapidly succumbed to the law of gravity. I lay there spread-eagle, with no breath in my lungs. I looked skyward and saw the vine tumbling down onto me in a big heap. It occurred to me at that moment that the vine needed to be connected to its roots for strength, for life.

If I had taken more time to check that vine, I probably wouldn't have fallen. I could have found out that the vine was not safe and that it was going to let me down. That vine failed me, but it was my own mistake.

It's the same in our spiritual life. Jesus says that he is the true vine and that he is our strength and life. Other things will look fun, strong, and non-threatening; but that may not be true. We have to check those things out carefully. They may just collapse under the strain of life. They can suck the very life and spirit out of you.

Jesus not only says that he is the true vine, he tells us that we are the branches. That means that we can actually be connected to him. We can hook up to all of what Jesus has to teach and offer. We can tap into the vine of life by knowing Jesus.

Take hold of Jesus and allow him to take hold of you. Hey! Have a fun ride.

—Rev. Stephen K. Doyal

Prayer: God, help us live as branches of the true vine. Take hold of us as we take hold of you. In Jesus' name, amen.

One 2 ONE

KISS MY Feet

James 5:15-16
Luke 7:37

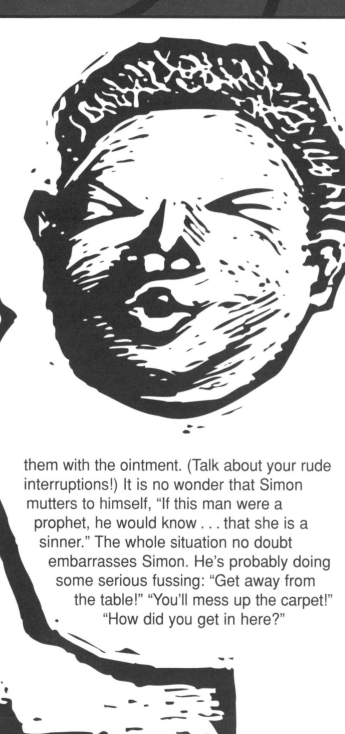

When When I think of examples of love, I think about an unnamed woman in the Bible. The Bible calls her a sinner. It is wild to me that this woman of all people could love Jesus so much.

I can just picture the scene when we first meet her. Jesus is eating dinner at the house of one of the Pharisees, which are the religious leaders of the day. The Pharisee is Simon, and I think that he brought Jesus over to impress him with a gourmet meal. Imagine a famous preacher coming to your house for dinner. How would the people around you act to welcome the preacher?

The woman shows up with jar of ointment. She stands behind Jesus and begins crying. Her tears are covering Jesus' feet. She wipes his feet with her hair and anoints

them with the ointment. (Talk about your rude interruptions!) It is no wonder that Simon mutters to himself, "If this man were a prophet, he would know . . . that she is a sinner." The whole situation no doubt embarrasses Simon. He's probably doing some serious fussing: "Get away from the table!" "You'll mess up the carpet!" "How did you get in here?"

Jesus uses the incident as an opportunity to teach Simon a lesson, beginning with a parable. Jesus is in tune with more than the obvious. To Simon, the woman is a sinner; an intruder, perhaps, on his nice dinner; someone to be treated as an outcast; someone whom no one wants to love or deal with. To Jesus, the woman is a confessing sinner, seeking forgiveness. Her actions tell him that she is sorry and ready to change. This is the best way she can think of to reach out to Jesus: throw herself at his feet and, by her actions, beg for mercy. It is a desperate cry from a desperate woman.

Surely, she must be embarrassed and ashamed. But where does she get the courage to come to Jesus despite all her sin? Isn't she afraid that he would kick her out of the house and reject her? The answer lies in her love for him. She shows her love by bowing at his feet. She knows she needs help and he forgives her.

We too can go to God and throw ourselves at God's mercy, and God will forgive us. Because God has forgiven us, we are asked to also forgive. If I have wronged a friend, I can follow the woman's example and place myself at his or her feet. If I have been wronged, I can be forgiving as Jesus is. Confession and forgiveness are essential to keeping friendships together. Can you picture it in your life?

—Duke Gatsos

Prayer: Holy God, thank you for your forgiveness. Give me the courage to confess my wrongs. Give me the humility to forgive others. In Jesus' name, amen.

One 2 ONE

LEAP OF *Faith*

Hebrews 11:1
James 1:5-6
Mark 11:22-23
1 Corinthians 16:13

There I was, standing thirty feet in the air, attached to a rope, standing on a platform. A good friend of mine was telling me, "Trust me and jump for the bar."

"Jump for the bar?" I asked. "You mean that trapeze bar that is about eighty feet in the air and about a hundred feet out in front of me?"

"Yes," came the answer. She also said that the bar was only about six feet above the platform and about five feet out. But that optical illusion psyched me out.

I was going through a high ropes course at Wildcat Mountain Wilderness Center, in New Jersey. I was visiting my friend, who put me through the course as a model for a group of students with whom she was working that day. So there I was—a model. I had to jump. I trusted my friend, and I knew the equipment that I was attached to would hold. I just needed a healthy dose of old-fashioned faith.

Our daily lives are like that as well. Sometimes we need a dose of faith. We know that God will hold us, and we trust that our friends and family will catch us if we fall. But making the first move is hard. Finding the faith to take a step off the edge is hard; but when we do it, that helps us grow. Don't let yourself get psyched out by

One 2 ONE

life's problems, look to God to psyche you up to work through them. When school is tough, when work is hard, when life decisions are difficult, when relationships are on the fritz, faith becomes that much more important.

As for me, I did make that jump. And I caught the bar. I have gone on to do much more in my life as well. My advice to you is look for chances to stretch your faith. God does not give us challenges that we cannot handle. And once we go through the tough times, we are better off. Remember that God is with us. The exciting news is that once we have faith that God will guide us through, we gain strength.

—Paul Harcey

Prayer: Faithful God, you say that even faith is a gift. I'm ready to accept that gift. Thank you for offering such a gift to me. In Jesus' name, amen.

One 2 ONE

LEARN TO Listen

> Luke 2:41-47
> Matthew 14:22-33
> Matthew 9:18

The 10,000 lakes of Minnesota are great for canoeing. When I was growing up, my favorite place to go on the lakes was the Boundary Waters Canoe Area (BWCA). I liked it not just for its amazing beauty but for the intensity as well. All of my senses would come alive in the BWCA. My back and hands would hurt from paddling, but my heart was warmed by the sight of a moose or the call of a loon. Water, trails, campsites, cooking—living itself was better there.

When author Douglas Wood visited the BWCA, he was inspired to write the book *Paddle Whispers.* In it, Wood encourages us to listen to the world around us. He says things such as "become silent," "pay attention." What great ideas! They tell me a lot. They remind me that we can pay attention to everybody and everything. You never know when or how God will speak to you, give you a nugget of truth, help you along your way. It could be in a sunset or sunrise; it could be in the wind blown pines or the wave-soaked rocks.

Jesus gave us an example to follow. He listened to people who came to him, and he responded to their needs. He listened to his disciples and responded to their questions. He listened to God and responded to the Lord's plan as well.

Jesus went away to pray. I am sure he did a lot of listening up on those mountaintops.

We would be wise to do the same. Good, effective listening to people takes a lot of energy, but the payoff is great. You will learn a lot. You will better understand people and learn how to be better understood. And people will respond to you because you listen.

Get away to listen. Learn to become a good listener to people. Practice listening for God in all that you do.

—Paul Harcey

Prayer: God, I'm listening. Are you speaking? Help me hear you in my life: in nature, in circumstances, in other people. In Jesus' name, amen.

One 2 ONE

LOOKING FOR THE *Light*

John 8:12
Matthew 5:14-16

I was sitting in my comfy apartment, watching a favorite TV show with my college roommate. The show was a bit suspenseful, and the atmosphere was right for it. Outside, it was dark and stormy; and inside, the suspense was building. Then, without warning, it became dark inside. With only about ten minutes left of our show, we lost our electricity. It was a shock. We would never know how the show ended.

After a few moments of whining, we calmed down. This was not that big of a deal. Instead, this was the time to do something—get some light. For this self-proclaimed gear head, finding light meant finding my camping lantern. We also had some candles around. The problem was we could not find a lighter or matches.

We turned our place upside-down looking for a flame. We were obsessed. I finally remembered that I had a lighter in my van. Out the door and into the rain, I went to find it.

With the lighter, we lit the candles and started to light the lantern. It needed a new mantle. (The mantle is the part that burns, as a wick does.) We tied a new one on and got it ready. Then we discovered that we had no gas left. I had a spare gas canister, and we started to change it. While putting in the new canister, I accidentally bent the needle that goes into the gas; so we had to try to straighten out the needle.

We finally got the lantern lit. It was very bright, as it was designed to be. It gave off light, the light we were seeking at all costs. It took a real struggle to get this light, and once we did, we knew we had it. This lantern lit up the whole room. We felt great that we had the light.

The funny thing was once we got the light, we just sat there and talked. It was not as if we needed the light to get some work done. We didn't do any reading; we didn't clean the place; we didn't play a game. We had just felt compelled to go on a mission to get light. We could have just as well stayed in the dark, but we *wanted* light. We *needed* light.

Are you on a mission to have the light of Jesus Christ in your life? With the Light of the World in your life, it is easier to see the joy of others, it is easier to see the right way to go, it is easier to see yourself and where Jesus is.

The Christian walk can sometimes be like my struggle to light my lantern. If you don't have the spark it takes to get the flame lit, find it—whatever it takes. When you run out of gas, you may have to do some maintenance on your faith. Just as I put on a new tank of gas, you may have to refill yours. Find the people in your life who can fill your tank. Find the Scriptures in the Bible that can fill your tank. Go to God to get your spirit refilled.

Walking in the light is not always easy. Sometimes you may be down to the light of just one match. In the darkness of the world, however, that can be enough to find your way. That can be enough for someone else to find his or her way. Keep the fire burning.

—Paul Harcey

Prayer: God, help us in the search to find your light. And help us to see around us because of your light. In Jesus' name, amen.

One 2 ONE

MARTHA OR Mary?

As I was growing up, my sisters and I always had to clean the kitchen after dinner. No matter how much work had to be done, my twin sister would always find a way to get out of it by paying attention to my parents and doing something else for them.

As I have grown older, I continue to work and put things in order. In planning events, whether it is a huge mission project or a simple meal with a friend, I find myself worrying about the details, which sometimes cause me to miss fully participating in the event.

In college, as my friends were out playing together, I was usually in the dorm room, working hard trying to get that A—believing that this was the thing that would make the biggest difference in my future. Yes, I did get those A's, but there was something more important that I missed. I missed spending time with my friends. I missed ice cream runs in the middle of the afternoon and those late-night doughnut runs that kept my friends awake while doing their papers. I can never recapture the time that I missed with my friends and the opportunities I could have learned from their experiences.

Just like Martha, I was too busy worrying about the work around me and not about what mattered most: the lessons that Christ has to offer. We can continue to focus on the chaos of a situation; but if we do, we will miss the incredible power of our Savior and the cross.

The next time you are in the middle of something, take a minute to ponder a question or two. Who do you think you're more like—Martha or Mary? Are you taking the time to stop and enjoy the journey? the beauty? Are you taking time to meet Jesus in your circumstances? Or are you too busy just getting things done? Take the time to be with Jesus. It is the most important thing you can do.

—Amanda Goins

Prayer: God, so much needs to be done. Chaos surrounds me. I want to sit at your feet so that you can teach me. I want to trust you to take care of everything else. In Jesus' name, amen.

One 2 ONE

OLD RUNDOWN *Shacks*

> Hebrews 12: 1-3

While working in Middle Tennessee on a mission project, I was given the responsibility of securing lumber donations for building projects. I would often drive country highways in search of reusable wood. Occasionally, I would pass some rundown barns. If you have ever driven in the country, I'm sure you've seen the kind of buildings I'm talking about; they dot the countryside. These shacks lean to one side, seeming to defy the law of gravity. They are usually colored a weather-worn shade of gray or a failing, dusty red. Various slats are missing and hay spills through the cracks between boards.

I was just a visitor to the area for the summer and didn't understand what function these buildings serve until the day I talked to an owner of a particularly rundown barn. I asked the man if we could come tear down the shack and use the lumber to build onto the homes of people who needed it.

He said, "I'm sorry son, but we use that old barn to store our hay." At first I was a little surprised. From my perspective, the barn had seen its better days; and I had a great use for the lumber. Later, as I spent more time in the country, I came to appreciate these barns. They serve as a connection to a traditional way of life. They are highway signs that represent a lifestyle of humility and hard work. I have borrowed some of this lifestyle from the experience I had in the country and have grown closer to God because of it. I appreciate those old barns for reminding me of another side of life.

Tradition gets a bad rap these days. People complain about having to conform to "boring, old church routine." But most of those traditions are there for a reason—not just to irritate us. It's helpful for us to try to understand why the traditions are there before we jump to tear down the old ways. It may be a little more work, but it's a response of love.

At the very least, we can learn about the lives of "the great cloud of witnesses" who have gone on before and who are precious in God's eyes. At the most, we might learn to adopt a part of the traditions as we grow. Either way, we can get closer to God by building up in love rather than tearing down in the name of progress. Sometimes seeing an old barn, singing an old hymn, or hearing an old story helps us to get in touch with the God of all time.

—Duke Gatsos

Prayer: You are the author of my faith. Perfect my faith by teaching me about love. Help me treat my elders with respect. Give me compassion for them and a desire to understand why they stand for certain things. May I learn something about you from what I see and hear in them. Amen.

One 2 ONE

ONE BREAD CRUMB, *Please*

| Matthew 15:21-28 |

Jesus says, "It is not fair to take the children's food and throw it to the dogs," when he and the disciples encounter a Canaanite woman. The woman has just begged Jesus to heal her daughter, who has been possessed by a demon. The woman replies: "Lord, that's true; but even dogs get the crumbs that fall from their owner's table."

Jesus just called this woman and her daughter dogs! Had this been me, I would be upset. I doubt that I would have the patience to say to Jesus, "Yes, Lord, but even us dogs have to eat sometime. And if I don't get the whole loaf of bread, I'm going to scrounge under your table and find some crumbs."

This woman causes Jesus to make a critical decision. Should he ignore her simply because she is not a Jew, or should he recognize her great faith and grant her request?

Can you imagine the disciples standing around, silent and on edge? The woman, with tears streaking her dirty face, is crumpled on the ground around Jesus' feet, pleading for his mercy. And Jesus is standing there, thoughtfully pondering this woman's plea. He is sent "only to the lost sheep of the house of

Israel." Should he heal this Canaanite's daughter? His answer, of course, you know. Jesus answers, "Woman, great is your faith! Let it be done for you as you wish."

Can we have faith like this woman? Often, when we are faced with adversity, our faith seems to dwindle and dissipate. For brief moments, we become very human, denying God because we think that we know better. We feel that if we left the situation up to God and lived by faith through confrontation, nothing would happen. Our humanness takes over at the very moment that we should be dropping to our knees at Christ's feet and crying out, "Allow me just a crumb from your table, Lord!" Christ's answer to each of us will be, "You have great faith! Your request is granted."

—Matthew W. Charlton

Prayer: Give me the faith of this woman who dares to come to you with her deepest needs. Thank you for being a giving, loving God. In Jesus' name, amen.

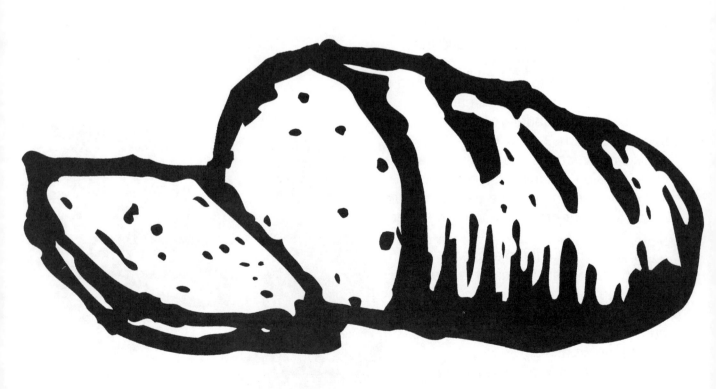

One 2 ONE

> ### John 14:6-14

The score was 19 to 17. Brett and I were playing one on one at the blacktop court at Dover Center Park. My boom box was playing backup music, but we were focused on the game and didn't really hear it. The winning score was 21, and this time Brett had the ball and the lead. He was bouncing the ball up and down, sounding out his rhythm as he decided his next shot. The hollow tang of the ball began to hypnotize me. But as he started his move—dribble right, crossover left, cross back right, lay up—I was ready, because I knew his moves. I stole the ball on the second crossover.

We continued that game back and forth until somebody won, but there was always another game. We would hit the parks, his driveway, school courts, church gyms—anyplace with a hoop. Sometimes he won; sometimes I won. It didn't really matter. We

came to know each other's moves so well that we could predict where each of us would be and be there before the other was ready. Eventually, we had to come up with new moves to improve and keep the game exciting.

I have found that Jesus loves to play one on one. I meet him at a certain time on the court of my choosing. We banter back and forth with some idle talk and then get down to business. I throw out a question, and Jesus responds with a truth. I wrestle with the truth for a while and run it through my life.

We challenge each other back and forth with ideas until I get tired. Jesus never does. I finish our time together enriched by the fact that he is greater than I am. I feel privileged to play with one so great. The fact that he allows me to be on the court with him amazes me. I love to watch his moves. He responds to me with so much grace and understanding. When I leave the court, I realize that I don't have to have all the answers. I find peace in the fact that he wants to spend some time with me just as I am. And just like in hoops, I get better the more I show up to play.

—Duke Gatsos

Prayer: Active God, let's play one on one. I'll meet you each day. I'll throw you my concerns, questions, thanks, and praise. I'll welcome your loving responses. In Jesus' name, amen.

One 2 ONE

PEANUT BUTTER & Jelly

Matthew 10:8b-10

I was making a peanut butter and jelly sandwich for breakfast one morning. I know that PB&J for breakfast sounds strange, but I was fresh out of raisin bran. Anyway, every time I make a PB&J sandwich, I'm stuck with the problem that probably plagues most PB&J sandwich makers. There really is no easy solution. The problem is knowing which product to put on first. Do you put on the peanut butter first or the jelly?

You see, here's the dilemma: When making a PB&J sandwich, you want to be conservative by using only one spreading utensil. Washing dishes after making a

simple PB&J seems like such a waste of time. Therefore, you should dirty only one utensil. So, would you rather have jelly smearings in your peanut butter jar or little chunks of peanut butter discoloring your jelly?

I've tried everything to combat this pestilence of peanut butter and jelly cross-pollination. I've wiped the knife on the remaining piece of bread to remove excess product. This doesn't work, because soft bread simply does not make a good wiping tool. I've thought about licking the knife clean but that seemed to be too disgusting, especially if other people plan on using the peanut butter or jelly in the future.

I've thought about wiping the knife clean with a paper towel, but that is a waste of resources for a simple sandwich. Where does it end? How can I solve this most difficult of problems? Which do I want: peanut butter-laden

SMOOTHY peanut butter

GRAPE JELLY

jelly or grape-flavored peanut butter? This just blows my mind!

Perhaps, I am being a little too obsessive about this peanut butter and jelly thing. Maybe I've gone just a little bit overboard with my maniacal ravings about a silly sandwich. Is it all that important? Probably not, but who wants a disgusting sandwich?

Every day there are little things that bother us. That is part of being human. Little things such as how to properly carry your backpack, the appropriate width of a belt for a certain outfit, whether to tuck or untuck your shirt, whether to smile at that cute girl in the next row. All of these little things can get jumbled up in your mind, making you so worried that your brain feels as if it is going to explode.

We can learn from Jesus Christ not only about his saving nature but about how to live without all this garbage floating around in our head. Jesus sets the example. The only things he had were a robe and some sandals. He didn't carry any money, didn't have a backpack to carry around all of the books of Jewish Law, and he didn't worry. When he sent the disciples out to minister to the lost sheep, Jesus gave this instruction: "You received without payment; give without payment. Take no gold, or silver, or copper in your belts, no bag for your journey, or two tunics, or sandals, or a staff; for laborers deserve their food."

So it is with us. We are called to simpler lives that are not full of unnecessary stuff. In giving this instruction to the disciples, Jesus was helping them focus on the task by removing what we consider necessary and replacing them with something priceless: faith that God will provide. Jesus reminds us not to worry over the little things, like my sandwich.

—Matthew Charlton

Prayer: Lord, help me to simplify my life. Open my heart to the message of Jesus Christ and to his healing. In Jesus' name, amen.

One 2 ONE

R E B E L WITH A *Clue*

Matthew 12:1-8
Luke 13:10-17
John 13:33-35

What makes a person a rebel? Some would say that a troublemaker is a rebel. Some would say that someone who smokes, fights, drinks, or takes drugs is definitely rebel material. Still others say that rebels are persons who do the opposite of what is expected of them. They might take the car without asking, skip class, or drop out of school. I say that people who rebel in these ways are rebels without a clue.

Jesus had the right idea when it came to going against the grain; he was a rebel with a clue. What made Jesus so powerful was that he knew his purpose. He did not come to break things, to steal, to vandalize property, or to show that he was angry with the world. He came to save the world. He came to stand up and be counted, to make a difference.

All through his life, Jesus stepped up to the plate. He came to bat for us; now it is our turn. They were going to stone a prostitute, but Jesus stood up for her. You can stand up for the new kid, the nerd, or the oppressed. Be an ally for someone who has none.

Jesus threw the moneychangers out of the Temple. You can make a stand for social injustice or wrong doings in the church. Jesus dedicated his life to the unwanted. Do you know someone who feels unwanted, someone who could use your touch and understanding?

Be a representative of Jesus. Do and say what Jesus would. Let your friends, your school, your church, and your family know what you believe in; then prove your beliefs. As you pray, ask God to give you opportunities to make a stand, to make a difference. God is asking us to be rebels with a clue.

—Paul Harcey

Prayer: God, make me a rebel with a clue for my family, friends, school and church. Give me the courage and desire to be your representative, acting and speaking as Jesus would. Give me opportunities to make a stand, to make a difference. In Jesus' name, amen.

One 2 ONE

SEEKING A Vision

John 14:6
Exodus 3:3-5
Ezekiel 36:24-27
Joel 2:28-29

As we stared at the fire and became entranced by its glow, my friend, of the Crow nation, was moved to tell me about his ancestors and their activities in Big Horn Mountains of Wyoming, where we were camping. He told me about his grandfather who had to go on a vision quest before he could become a warrior.

While the young man was expected to seek vision at some time, he could do so when he chose. Every so often the camp crier would ride through the village, calling for the young men to go to the mountains to seek a vision. All boys knew that to become a man, to gain purpose and direction for his life, vision was needed. To some people, the Great Spirit

had given the special ability to heal, while to others he gave the power to change battles or the outcome of some other event. Vision would help the initiate realize the closeness of the spirit world and his relationship to the power of the spirits.

At about age thirteen, my friend's grandfather decided that it was time to seek vision. He went to a holy man who prepared him for the ordeal. The holy man told him that at birth each Crow is given a sacred helper, who would be identified by his vision. If the helper was powerful, my friend's grandfather would live to be a wise elder of his tribe.

Next, the holy man directed him to the sweat lodge. He said that the steam that rose from water poured on the hot rocks represented the image of First Maker. The sweat that the boy's body would produce was sacred and cleansed both body and soul.

After that the holy man instructed the boy to go into the mountains to find a sacred place. The boy was to divest himself of his clothing and purify himself in the smoke of pine needles to eliminate the human smell. He stayed in the mountains for four days without food or water. As he prayed for vision, he pierced his body—as he was directed by the holy man—as a sacrifice to the creator, while he pleaded for blessing.

After seeking vision, my friend's grandfather returned from the mountains. Some nations tell their dreams to a holy man or their grandparents, but the Crow do not tell their dreams. My friend's grandfather did, however, make a shield that symbolized his dream and its power to the vision seeker.

In the Bible, mountains and hills are often spiritual places. Moses has a direct vision with God on a mountain. Moses talks with God. God gives Moses the power to change the outcome of many events. By the power of God, Moses started and stopped plagues in Egypt, he led his people out of the land, and he turned water into blood and sticks into serpents.

For the Crow, sweat symbolizes purity; in the Bible, blood is the sign of purity. The early Hebrews confessed their sins to God and sacrificed a lamb as a sin offering. Christians confess sins and take Jesus Christ as their sacrificial Lamb. His shed blood brings our purity before God.

Our traditions may differ, but God is the God of all. The Great Spirit is the center of life. God has prepared all the cultures of the world to be ready to hear the saving message of Jesus Christ. By that message and by the power of God, we are made pure and we are empowered to change the world.

—Dennis Harcey

Prayer: God, you are an amazing creator. You created all kinds of people and prepared each of us to be reconnected with you and your world. Thank you for mountains, for sweat, for hills, for blood. Thank you for Jesus. Amen.

One 2 ONE

SLIPPERY WHEN Wet

> James 1:2-4
> Ephesians 6:10-20

If you do not have any experience with North Carolina clay, let me give you some insight. It is slippery when wet. A lot of rain had fallen the week I worked in North Carolina as a raft guide/ropes course facilitator. As part of our duties, we would have to gather fire wood for campers. We took the van over the hill to fill it up with wood. On the way back, I was taught a lesson in perseverance.

The back of the hill had no gravel on it. It did have nice ruts. But the ruts were in some of that wet, nasty, slick clay. We quickly got stuck on the way out. We could not get the van over the hill. First, we tried speed. We backed up as far as we could and gunned it. Speed did not work.

Then we tried the old trick of letting out some air in the tires. This gives the tires more traction, and it usually works; not this time.

Next, we started putting boards down for traction. But this really didn't get us anywhere either.

We had been at it about an hour or so. Tempers were about to go. It was not a good scene. We even started talking about giving up and getting some help. We did not give up though; we persevered.

Finally, we used rocks, boards, and sticks. We pushed, gunned, and inched our way up the hill. All and all, it took almost two hours; but we did get out.

Many times in my life I have felt as if I were stuck. Do you ever feel as if there is no way out, and you just want to give up? Don't give up. Let some air out, use rocks for a strong hold, and push and inch your way out. Being able to persevere is a great quality to have. Giving more than you thought you had, not quitting when you have trouble in a relationship, keeping your energy up for long-term commitments, or taking just a few more steps when you really want to quit are all examples of digging deep and persevering.

Job is a prime example of someone persevering. He was a man of God who never wavered. Job persevered

through not only pain and the loss of everything he had, but even through his friends speaking against him. Job endured a lot for the sake of the Lord and was given two fold back what was lost.

Check out what else the Bible has to say about perseverance.

—Paul Harcey

Prayer: Patient God, when I feel like giving up, give me the courage to keep going. When I'm tempted to quit my relationships and responsibilities, give me the strength to stay loving and committed. In Jesus' name, amen.

One 2 ONE

SPEAKING GOD'S Language

Philippians 4:6,7

I recently went to the bookstore to find a book to help me learn how to publish a web page on the Internet. Some of the youth in my church asked about getting a page together, and I found out that we could get free space on the World Wide Web.

I wanted to play a few games over the Internet too. Not fully trusting my ability to work with the computer, I made sure that I got a book that was easy to understand. After reading the first chapter, though, I knew that I had made the right choice.

Learning how to write a web page was really simple. All I was going to have to do was learn a new language. The language for web pages is HTML, which stands for Hypertext Markup Language. Don't let the name fool you, the language is really very simple. In fact, I was able to make my own cool web page in a matter of hours. By no means is that page exciting, but it will be after I do some more work and study.

As we learn more words and sentences, a new language becomes our own. The language that we use to speak with God is called prayer. Like HTML, prayer is simple; but it is difficult to master.

I have recently accepted the challenge to take prayer more seriously. The most

rewarding benefit of my new commitment was that I learned some new ways to pray. I learned to sit and listen to God. I learned how to offer my time in silence to God. I praised God for aspects of God's character that I seldom thought about. I was learning new levels of a language.

Prayer is miraculous, because God changes our hearts when we open ourselves up in prayer. I was giving time and energy to God, but I was the one reaping

the benefits. I would leave my prayer hour with a new outlook on life. I became a better disciple, because I knew that God cared about me. As I listened, God expressed love for me day after day.

Don't get me wrong, simple prayer is one of the great gifts we can give. God will accept any prayer on any terms. I am thankful for the opportunity to give that gift. However, I know that I can benefit greatly from more time spent in God's presence. The more I try to live out my faith, the more I need God's power.

We access God's power through prayer. Why do we forget to deepen our prayer lives? Why do we let insignificant, temporary things steal our time away from an eternal investment?

I challenge you to take your understanding of prayer to another level. God loves to hear from us. God wants to speak to us, mostly to express love to us. By the way, while it is easy to write a web page, posting it to the Internet is an entirely trying ordeal. I am thankful that God gives us direct access. We don't have to log on to get God's attention.

—Duke Gatsos

Prayer: Thank you, God, for always being available to hear our prayers. Teach us your language as we strive develop a friendship with you. Remind us of your great love for us. In Jesus' name, amen.

One 2 ONE

T A K E ME TO THE *Edge*

> ## Matthew 4:21-22

W hile riding my bike one day when I was about seven, I passed an object glittering in the sun. I picked it up, not recognizing it as a razor blade, since I had not started to shave yet. I put it in my pocket and thought nothing of it for a couple of hours until I put my hand into my pocket and pulled out a bloody finger. The bad thing about razor cuts is that they seem to just keep bleeding. I sucked on my finger, trying to make it stop. Eventually, the bleeding stopped.

A few years later, a couple of friends and I had decided to go rappelling one day. Basic rappelling is when you slide backward down a rope over a cliff. You can push off the rock and let the rope slide through your hands as you go down. I that know it sounds difficult. And I was thinking, "How could these guys be my friends and be so dumb at the same time?"

Since they were my friends and I was feeling peer pressure, I found myself on the top of the cliff about 2 million feet in the air (or about 150 feet). Well, after I had thought about it for a few minutes, not wanting to talk myself out of it, I stepped off. As you can tell, I lived. In fact, it was a rather exciting experience. The first step was the hard part.

A third, seemingly unrelated event occurred when I was about thirteen. My father had been suffering from a blood illness related to alcoholism. I did not understand how serious it was. He eventually died from it.

I remember going to school for the first time after he died. Oddly, I remember staring at the big double doors into the school. I had to go back in there and face everybody without my dad. It was hard enough before, and now it seemed impossible. It was hard to go in; but if I had stood there and thought about it, I would have run back home.

So what do these things have in common? They all reflect the edge. The edge is that space in time when you are confronted with a choice. It is that place where you end up on one side of the razor blade or the other—there is no middle ground. It's not comfortable; it's not easy. You have to decide whether to go on or to take a step back. The longer you think about it, the more likely you are to freeze up and never choose or to let it choose you. It is a defining moment in time. It helps shape your life. Sometimes you have to jump over that cliff, even if at first it does not make sense. Still, you never need to go without a rope.

Now, Jesus is my rope. He holds me fast as I choose my way through life. I know that I can do anything, because I trust that God will take me across the edge. Facing the edge is impossible for me without Jesus.

When in your life have you been taken to the edge? What or who did you trust to take you across the edge.

—Duke Gatsos

Prayer: Jesus, be my rope. Hold me fast as I choose my way through life. I know that I can do anything when I trust that you will take me across the edge. By the power of the Holy Spirit, amen.

One 2 ONE

THE FISHING Hole

> John 14:26
> Luke 12:8-12
> Ephesians 6:11-17

The mountains of southwestern North Carolina are home to many great trout streams. The water moves fast and is always cold. The mountains are high and old. There are many green, deep, plush valleys that have seen many centuries of rain and water to shape them. In the tall poplar and pine, these mountains hide some of the great spots in this world. This is a beautiful area.

Imagine yourself out fishing in this area. First, you find your favorite spot, your secret fishing hole. The water is deep there as the stream widens out. It is very cold, so you put on your waders. Now is the time to head out into the water and start casting. You are very careful because of the slippery rocks under your feet. If you were to slip and fall, your waders would fill with water and drag you down. The current is strong—just standing there can be hard at times—so you have to know where to step. You have to know where the sure footing is.

The most serene, beautiful, quiet place can be filled with danger if you are not careful. A place that is perfect in God's creation can be the most special place. This very same place can be deadly. With one

One 2 ONE

wrong move, one false step, you can be caught and dragged downstream. The fast stream can carry you away; the cold brutal water can take its toll on you in the blink of an eye. One minute you can feel secure; the next, you are in grave trouble.

What are the slippery rocks of your life? What do you see in your life that could cause you to fall in to the water and drift away? If you are not careful in your daily life, what might happen to you? Do you give in to peer pressure? Do you fight with your brothers, sisters, or parents? Do you hurt those around you?

We must go into the world, into the stream that can be dangerous. God helps us with our steps. We can call on God to help us find our talents. We need to call on the Lord to give us strength to go into the stream. These are the gifts that God gives us to get us through life.

So, go explore. Find out what is in the stream, what is around the next bend, what surprises God has for you. Develop your talents, share what you have, and have fun while you are out fishing.

—Paul Harcey

Prayer: Guiding God, lead me around slippery rocks. Watch my feet for me. Save me if I happen to drift away. Free me from any traps in my world. Thank you for caring. In Jesus' name, amen.

One 2 ONE

THE INSIDE-OUT *Exercise*

> Romans 12:1-2

My husband and I have a membership at the YMCA. We joined to increase our exercise so that we can stay healthy and keep our muscles toned to avoid what we call "old-age sagging." Trying to get into the routine of exercise has been hard and has taken a lot of commitment to see it through. My husband is doing a great job at keeping his commitment to exercise. I am finding it hard to stay on a routine while being a wife and mom and working full time in ministry. I keep telling myself that I must prioritize and get my life in order so that I can make time for this necessary aspect of good living. Right?

Well, partly right. I have come to realize that I had everything out of order. I was putting too much emphasis on exercising the wrong part of my life. Sure, physical exercise is critical and something that I should do to maintain a healthy lifestyle. But shouldn't I consider my spiritual fitness as well? During this whole time of committing, promising, and even attempting to set goals and meet them, I didn't once spend the time needed on committing myself to exercising my spirituality. I discovered that I could use some routine there too.

What about my prayer life? What about my study life? What about worship in my life? What about service to others? I began asking myself many of these tough questions and realized that what I need first, over anything else, is to exercise from the inside out. I need to establish a spiritual exercise routine, working on the spiritual disciplines in order to help me be a better witness and servant of Christ.

Inside-out exercises help us become fuller and richer in our understanding of Christ and who he is in our lives. We can share Christ to the fullest only when we are seeking to be a healthy follower ourselves. Practicing the disciplines such as prayer, study, worship, and service can help to change our insides. Our inside change will help us to change our communities, our schools, our work places, our communities, and our families—all for the purpose of glorifying God in the highest.

So, I'm setting new goals in my life. Yeah, physical fitness is still important; but more of my energy has shifted to working on my spiritual fitness. I am preparing for a new journey with Christ as I seek to do my inside-out exercises on a routine basis.

—Trish Pulley

Prayer: God, will you be my spiritual trainer? Will you give me the direction and discipline I need? Will you pick up for me when I can't do it on my own? Thank you for spiritual strength. In Jesus' name, amen.

One 2 ONE

THE LOST *Sheep*

Luke 15:4-7

John 10:11-18

Psalm 139

Teachers can make it awfully hard to get an *A*. The toughest assignments often have a lot of little parts to them. Sometimes your assignment can look like this:

> 10 points for complete sentences
> 20 points for being typed
> 10 points for being long enough
> 25 points for the choice of topic
> 20 points for using the library
> 15 points for being on time

You get the point. Making the grade on this kind of assignment can seem next to impossible. Sometimes students need to make choices such as handing in the assignment a little late in order to be able to type it or using three library books instead of four. Students make tough decisions and need to make judgments regarding their time and ability in order to get the most points.

In Luke, Jesus tells a parable of the lost sheep. "Which of you, having a hundred sheep and losing one of them, does not leave the ninety-nine in the wilderness and go after the one that is lost until he finds it?"

If Jesus had asked a group of shepherds in shepherd school this question, what do you think the response would be? It sounds like a trick question. Ninety-nine sheep out of a hundred is a really good percentage, isn't it? It's a solid *A*. And who would risk leaving the ninety-nine unattended sheep for one wandering, dimwitted sheep? What if eight

more sheep left the unattended flock while the shepherd searched for the one? Then the percentage would really be down—even close to a B. What if eighty more of them left and wandered into a dangerous gorge? The shepherd would be unemployed after that kind of a bad day at work.

But Jesus doesn't cast us as the shepherd in the story. Each of us is that lost sheep. If I were the lost sheep, I would be grateful for such an attentive and loving shepherd. God the shepherd always seeks the lost sheep and will always gently and happily carry us home. Seeking and finding and rejoicing with the retrieved lost sheep is something that God, a truly Good Shepherd, never tires of doing. God doesn't count the percentages and cut corners but seeks, finds, and rejoices over finding all the lost all the time.

—Sharri Larson

Prayer: Thank you, God, for seeking me, finding me, and cherishing me as part of your flock. Help me to see all those around me as your cherished ones too. In Jesus Christ's name, amen.

One 2 ONE

T H E SETTING *Sun*

Matthew 10:29-31

Romans 8:28

Romans 12:6-8

It had been a long day. I was driving I-24 West someplace between Chattanooga and Nashville, Tennessee. It had been a great day. I had taken a youth group out rappelling. We all had a good experience and I was on my way home.

But I noticed something. It was something that I had seen many times. In fact, it happens every day all around the world—sunsets. But this sunset was different than others I had seen. The clouds had formed is such a way as to only leave a horizontal slot from which the sun was beaming

out. It was as if the sun had become a long, thin bar. At this point, the sun was not low enough to become red; so it was a whitish yellow light coming out of a hole. Now this in itself was really cool. Like I said, I had never seen such a thing as this. It was a one of a kind. Then I started to think about other sunsets I have seen. I had seen lots of really cool sunsets.

One time I was driving with a friend while a storm was brewing. In summertime in Nashville, we get a lot of thunderstorms. Nashville summers are hot and humid; and in the late afternoon through the evening hours, it can rain on almost any day. My friend and I could see that off in the distance a storm had started. It took up most of the left part of the sky. The sky was very dark, and we could see the rain. The other side of the sky was clear and calm. What made this an

eye opener was the fact that the sun was the divider. The sun was cut in half by the thunderstorm. The scene was dramatic, inspiring, and powerful. The sky was dark, powerful, and storming on one side and red, orange, blue, and white on the other.

Another memorable sunset happened when I went skiing one time in France. The ski village that was about 6000 feet up. Out of the window I could see a snow-covered, jagged mountain reaching up with its exposed rocks. I could also see part of our village. Right in the center of my view was a chair lift. All of this was backlit by a bright red sunset. Lots of clouds were in the sky that night, but it was not cloudy. They were little clouds, puffy and rolling. They seemed to be in uniform lines stretching across the sky. And all of those clouds were reflecting that deep red of the setting sun. The scene was picturesque and serene, giving me a sense of wonder, awe, and peace.

It struck me how sunsets are like God's children. As children of God, each of us is different. Some of us are made to be big and glorious and inspiring. Some of us are made to be dramatic and to carry a point. Most of us seem to be everyday, ordinary sunsets. God creates us to be different, just like the sunsets. No two sunsets are the same; no no two people are the same.

I used the word *ordinary* on purpose, because there is actually nothing ordinary about a sunset. Because sunsets occur everyday, we think of them as ordinary. But to think that way would be a trap. A sunset is a huge production. Sunsets can be spectacular. When we see an impressive one, we are inspired to thank God. But God's effort is in every ordinary sunset.

You too are a huge production. So is each person God has put on this earth. We may seem ordinary, but we are not. We each have much to offer. Each of us is a little different; each of us has different ideas. Each of us, like the sunset, is a one-of-a-kind gift from God. Each sunset can be a reminder of God's glory. Each person on earth is also a reminder of God's glory—even more than a sunset—because each person is created in God's image.

Who inspires you to thank God? Tell him or her. Who looks at you and thanks God for you? Next time you see a sunset, thank God for the lovely sight and for the reminder of how unique you really are.

—Paul Harcey

Prayer: Thank you, God, for sunsets. Thank you for the people in my life who are as unique and spectacular as each sunset. Help me to treat the people in my life with the wonder that you do. In Jesus' name, amen.

One 2 ONE

THE TRUE *Team*

Romans 12:4-8

The morning was glorious, beautiful, perfect. I was walking down the wood chip path that worked its way around the lake like a ribbon on a package holding the gift that was this perfect day. The sky was a rich blue, the leaves were a rainbow of fall colors, and the water was still and peaceful. It was one of those days that I want to suspend in time. I praise God for giving me such a wonderful day.

The sound of silence and solitude in the early morning was slowly broken. I began to listen, trying to make out who or what dared to disturb my day. Slowly I figured out what the sounds were. "Stroke, stroke, stroke" is what I heard. Out of the crisp fog of the morning, I saw a crew team skating across the mirrored lake in as perfect unity as my surroundings. I stopped to watch and marvel at the sight. God seemed to be taking care of me once more. In this day that seemed made for me was a lesson that was meant for me.

I stood in the early morning air and learned a little about a crew team. This team consisted of one woman and eight men. As I was standing there, something occurred to me. This was a true team. It had a coach back on shore guiding and nurturing the nine members, the woman was calling cadence, and the men were working together in unison. The team must have wanted to be good,

to win, to have fun, since they were out on the water at 6:30 a.m. The team worked out together and practiced together. They probably talked about their dreams and goals as individuals and as a team.

Their commitment is inspirational. They show us that if we want something as a team, we must be willing to pay the price. The crew team knows what they want and how to get it. If we are to do the same, we must talk to one another, support one another, and be willing to meet the challenge. God is our coach, training us on shore, guiding us, supporting us, and getting us ready.

Our teams are families, youth groups, school groups, and others. It is up to us to support one another, help one another, and be there for one another when one member is in need. Our goals should be then to listen to our coach, call a good cadence that others can follow when we are leaders, and to work hard and with one another when we are followers. All three are important parts of being part of God's team.

—Paul Harcey

Prayer: God, you are my coach in life. I want to follow you, work well with others for your purposes, and give my all in all I do. In Jesus' name, amen.

One 2 ONE

THREE LITTLE PIGS
Eternal

Matthew 7:24-28

Dateline: May 7, 1988, Fort Lauderdale Florida—Yesterday the house of Mr. Samuel T. Gottwald took its final slip into disaster as it was swallowed up by a 30-yard sinkhole. Gottwald's house had been on the verge of the sinkhole for the last 20 days.

"It was just a matter of time," Mr. Gottwald said, as he watched his most prized property slide, tumble, and crash into the ever-widening pit.

Mrs. Gottwald commented, "At least it was a gradual thing, and we were able to get out most of our belongings before it all went."

Mrs. Gottwald's optimism was not shared by her husband. "This is really going to set us back. It is like watching $150,000 falling into a hole. It'll take me years to even get close to rebuilding."

The local land surveyors commented, "He took the risk by putting his house there. We told him of the other disasters in the area. He was so excited to buy that he never listened to us."

Fort Lauderdale lawyers seem to back up the story of the surveyors. "Mr. Gottwald is going to have to cut his losses. I would hate

to be in his shoes, but maybe he should have thought more when he first started building."

Jesus calls wise those who build their lives on rock. We often think of our faith as something spiritual or emotional, something that moves around and is not really built on anything. What does Jesus mean? Surely, he doesn't want a bunch of immobile stonefaces in his church, does he?

Maybe God wants both from us. Perhaps we are to start with an unshakable foundation. Then, after we are sure of where we stand, we can build a more flexible structure that bends as we grow. In order to follow Jesus' command to "go and make disciples of all nations" we must be mobile. Still, we must also be unshakable in order to convey a message to others. We must have something to stand upon so that this world does not swallow us up into nothingness, into the sinking sand.

Any good builder will find a good place to build, then lay the foundation, and then build the rest of the structure. We are to do the same. Jesus is the foundation, the rock; and you are the rest of your structure. Once you know that, you can start building. You can put together your faith according to what the Bible has to say, your experience with other strong Christians, and your experience with God. You can start letting others know what you are doing and why; you can reach out to others and put your faith in action. You will never have all of the answers, so don't wait around to try to find them.

Get out there, stand on your foundation, and let the world know that you stand on the rock.

—Duke Gatsos

Prayer: Dear God, thank you for Jesus as the strong foundation of my faith. Show me how to build on that foundation so that my faith stays strong through everything that hits my life. Be my protection and comfort. In Jesus' name, amen.

One 2 ONE

TO BOLDLY GO

Numbers 13:25-33

Not to brag, but I was fast when I was in high school—very fast. I ran a 4.7 second 40-yard dash, fast enough to give me the honor of being the Inter-Mountain Athletic Conference Fastest Lineman of the Year in 1982. I tell you this so that you can appreciate the force with which I hit a clothesline on one fateful day.

Back then, I usually traveled on my trusty bike. But this day I found myself on foot. Walking made a short cut appealing. I knew that I could cut off about six blocks of walking if I just slipped across a particular backyard instead of following the street. I had stayed too long at my friend's house already, and time was of the essence. Staying out of trouble was a high priority.

As I cut across the yard, I encountered a typical privacy fence: wooden and so tall that I couldn't see over it. I climbed the fence and briskly hopped down on the other side. What happened next was like a scene out of a scary movie. My feet had barely hit the ground when I heard a dog. This was not merely a dog; it was a beast. It was a snarling, vicious, man-eating creature. Or at least that is what it sounded like.

I didn't hesitate or look back. I just knew that I could beat him to the other side of the yard, and then I would be home free. After all, I was the Inter-Mountain Athletic Conference Fastest Lineman of the Year. I was out of the starting blocks and in high gear before that pooch knew what was going on. He had a better chance of catching a car than catching me. He was nipping at my heels, though, as I began to pull away.

As I was busy leaving the hound in my dust and looking across the yard at my impending escape, I never even saw it. That clothesline caught me just below the nose on my upper lip. I am not positive, but I believe that my momentum caused me to do an entire flip before landing on my back, staring up at the sky. I was stunned, but I was cautious enough to know that I was a goner for sure. That dog would smell the blood and come finish me off. Amazingly, the dog just stopped and looked at me. I guess he had never seen a stupid human trick before. Then I saw the dog for the first time—all six inches tall of him. Somehow, he had sounded so much bigger.

Without a doubt, this world contains some truly dangerous things—things worthy of our fear. Our cities are bad, schools have shootings,countries are at war. Crime, neglect, and other bad things are going on out there. As Christians, we can decide whether we will be dominated by fear or dominated by faith.

Fear serves a purpose in our lives. But the usefulness of fear is far surpassed by the value of our faith. Had I taken some time to understand that the scary hound was truly no threat, I could have saved myself a lot of pain. When we put our faith in the Lord and understand that God is in control, fear does not have to grip our lives and we can save a lot of pain.

Many scary things are out there, but letting fear rule our lives is not the answer. Where your heart begins to fail, make the Lord your refuge. We are weak, but our God is strong.

—Reverend Stephen K. Doyal

Prayer: God, when I feel fear, give me faith. Let me see your control so that fear can't grip me. Be my refuge. I know that when I am weak, you are strong. In Jesus' name, amen.

One 2 ONE

TO DIE For

John 20:1-18
Romans 5:6-11
1 Peter 2:9-10

The sign said, "Join us at Easter Breakfast, 8–10 a.m. It's to die for!" The sign was hung on the church door a few weeks before Easter, announcing a fundraiser for the youth group.

To die for—People use that phrase to describe how wonderful something is, how great it tastes, how well worth time it is to do. We know what it means; it's a phrase used to pay a high compliment.

The sign for the Easter breakfast catches people's attention because we've heard the phrase before. The sign claims that the meal will be really good—worth our time and money.

The sign is also ironic and kind of humorous. We know that our Easter story is a story of a real death. We know that Easter is about the true act of God forgiving our sins through Christ's death on the cross. The Resurrection isn't amazing unless we believe in Christ's *actual* death. This is the Good News of our faith—that God gives life to what is dead. We know that God considered humans—of all things—something important enough "to die for." We are also, in God's eyes, something "to rise for."

Perhaps the church should host two meals. The first should be a meal that is something "to die for." We would be reminded what Good Friday is

Join us at Easter Breakfast 8–10 a.m. IT'S TO DIE FOR!

really about—that even though we are sinful, ungrateful, often unfaithful, and certainly unworthy, Christ died for us.

Paul writes to the Romans, "For while we were still weak, at the right time Christ died for the ungodly." Despite who we are, Christ considers us "to die for." When we think about and understand our sin, we find that we are more grateful for the forgiveness. When we're really hungry, we are more thankful for food. The meal could focus on how much we need Christ and on how we need forgiveness.

The bigger meal would be the next one—the follow-up meal, three days later. There would be a huge, celebrating sign on the doors and joyful music bursting through the church's speakers: "Easter breakfast is *to rise for.*" That's what Christ did, after all. Our breakfast would be asserting that it's worth our while to get up. We know that we need to lift our eyes and pay attention. We can rise to the occasion. We can celebrate that God gives life to the dead and frees us from sin.

Having Christ die for us is one step—an incredible sacrifice based on God's love and not on our behavior. But the better part is that Christ rises for us, calling all things new, naming us as children of God, and resurrecting our sinful selves from death to life.

—Sharri Larson

Prayer: God, remind us to celebrate Easter every day, knowing that every day—even every moment—we are given new life, because Jesus Christ has died for our sins. As we die to our sins with Christ, let us also rise with Christ to new life. In Christ's name, amen.

WANDERING IN THE *Wilderness*

> Exodus 16:1-12
>
> Luke 4:1-13

Our church built a putt-putt golf course for the youth to use. One of the best holes is called Wandering in the Wilderness. Golfers begin by hitting the ball up a steep hill. The golf ball sails off the edge and lands on a slanted board filled with nails that are pounded in about every two inches. That board leads to the next level, and every ball must travel through this "nail wilderness" to reach the destination.

When the ball lands on this slanted wall, it bounces off the nails precariously, often taking sharp turns around some nails, slowly making its way. Golfers hope that the nails don't cause the ball to wander too far and end up a long way from the hole. Sometimes, if the ball hits the nails just right, the ball can end up on the other side from where it started. But no matter what happens, the ball does eventually reach the next level. One force keeps it going—gravity.

If our lives are the golf balls, then the nails are the everyday things that affect us: school, people, families, jobs, activities. When we're busy and balancing many different things, we feel as if we have no direction. Sometimes our days can be absolutely hectic, filled with so many activities that it's hard to remember where we're going next and what we need to do to prepare. Many students bounce from class to class, to a meeting, to sports, to home for supper, back to school for band, to church for a meeting. It can be very tiring, and it's easy to lose perspective.

In the midst all of these things, remember that we are children of God, called to serve God, reflect God's love, and tell others about Christ.

In our Christian lives, God is the gravity. God is always present, even when we wander. We can feel as if we're lost in the wilderness, trying to balance lots of commitments and make good decisions. But even as we bounce around all of the issues, demands, and people in our lives, we can be certain that God calls us. God doesn't give up. God wants all children to find their way home.

The Bible has several stories about wandering. God leads the people from slavery, with Moses as their leader. They wander for forty years in the wilderness. At times they are frustrated with the wandering and lose hope that God is providing for them. But God does provide, sustaining them with water and bread from heaven.

In another story, Jesus is in the wilderness being tempted for forty days by the devil. Even when he is promised kingship of all lands if he would worship the devil, Jesus says, "It is written, 'Worship the Lord your God, and serve only him.' " God sustains Jesus in the wilderness with hope and strength.

In our lives, for all of the different ways we feel as if we're wandering, we can be certain that God sustains us, calls us, and leads us home. We can be certain that the obstacles, interruptions, and commitments are not as strong as the hand of God our Creator pulling us home.

—Sharri Larson

Prayer: God, be my gravity. As I bounce around all of the issues, demands, and people in my life, pull me back to you. Be my home. When I feel like wandering, call me and lead me home. In Jesus' name, amen.

One 2 ONE

WHAT'S IT *Worth?*

> Romans 5:15-21
> Philippians 2:1-13

You go to a restaurant, order your meal, and eat it. You get your money out to pay; and the server tells you that instead of the set price, you should pay whatever you thought the meal is worth. What would you pay?

We might be quick to say that we would take the food for free and save the money. We might be ecstatic for getting something free and for not having to pay between three and four bucks for our meal. But that isn't what the server said. The server doesn't say to not pay anything. She clearly says to pay what you thought the meal is worth.

A restaurant in Minneapolis does this every Monday. It's called "Set-Your-Own-Price Night." Customers must pay the minimum of $5.00, but the meals are listed in the menu as between $8.00 and $10.00. The server brings the bill at the end of the meal, and diners are instructed to fill in the charge according to what they

believe the meal is worth. Whatever they write, they pay.

When I first found out about this restaurant, I was excited to go. At the time, I had just graduated from college and didn't have a job or much money. I thought that it would be the perfect restaurant for me and my budget. I excitedly visited and was surprised to find that that the rumors about setting my own price were true.

The only problem was that the meal was delicious. I loved every bite. I had more than enough to eat, and it was excellent. *Pay what it's worth is a trick,* I thought after the meal.

The food is great. Although I was given the choice of what to pay, I felt compelled to compliment the chef and pay even more than the menu price. I couldn't get that out of my head, either; I was so happy, I had no choice but to pay more. I was thankful and appreciative of the good food and service.

Most restaurants believe that they are the best judges of what the meal is worth. But this restaurant has been willing to give diners the power. Hungry people are thankful for a great meal, and the restaurant gains even more for trusting the people to decide the worth.

What would you pay for your faith in Jesus Christ? The gifts of grace and forgiveness are so huge, so immense that we cannot be thankful enough. We know that we can do nothing to "pay" God for what God has done for us. God gives us life and salvation. We are given God's only son Jesus Christ to die for our sins, and we are given forgiveness. The grace of God has no price; we enjoy all the gifts, but then are given a "bill" with no charges. It's

hard to know what to do when we're given so much, and not allowed to pay. We feel helpless.

But if we could, we would probably be like the diners on Set-Your-Own-Price Night. We would realize the great worth of all God's gifts. We would be appreciative, thankful, and we would want to compliment. We receive bountiful gifts from God. We receive all that we need. What is that worth to us? How can our lives be a reflection of the gratitude we feel?

—Sharri Larson

Prayer: Generous God, your gifts are priceless. Thank you for life and salvation. Thank you for all that I need. Help our lives be a reflection of our gratitude to you. In Jesus' name, amen.

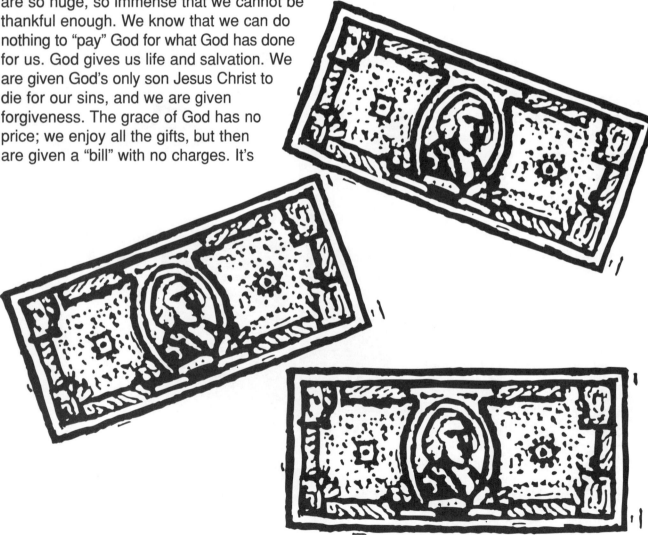

One 2 ONE

Isaiah 6:8-9
1 Samuel 3:1-10

One of the cyclists on our bicycle trip got sick one morning and was taken to the hospital. An adult counselor went with her, and I came back with our van at the end of the day to get them. The hospital was huge. I didn't know where they were or how to contact them. The nurses suggested that I page them. Even though I knew that the student who'd been sick was deaf, I knew that the adult counselor would hear the announcement. Besides, they had been there all day; and I knew that they'd be eager to leave.

I paged them several times over the next hour. I asked about them at every desk I could. I went to different wings of the hospital and even to a different building across the street, just in case they were somehow waiting there. I knew that they could not go anywhere without a vehicle, yet they did not answer any of my calls. More than ninety minutes had passed. Finally, they came out from an elevator door and asked me what had taken me so long.

Of course, I understood why the student hadn't heard the hospital intercom system. But the counselor that was with her had

She had simply gone to sleep to pass the time. She could hear perfectly, but she hadn't heard because she had been sleeping. The hospital intercom was not loud enough to wake her.

Have you ever had an experience like that? Things can be obvious, loud, intentional, and even right in front of us; and yet we miss it. Have you ever slept through a thunderstorm that was so loud the rest of your family was awake? Have you missed an important assignment in school because your mind wandered?

These things can happen to us in our faith too. The truth of God can be told to us, read to us, and shown to us. It can even be announced over loudspeakers. But if we are sleeping or zoning out, we will not hear.

It's never the case that God is not speaking. Sometimes we are more open to seeing and hearing God's truth than other times. Sometimes we can see the true gift of another person or the wisdom in something we read. We can be doing something away from our church and see the gospel shown through the kindness of a stranger or the goodness of a neighborhood caring for one another. Our eyes and ears can be filled with God's truth. Other times we miss the most obvious, because we are "sleeping" in one way or another.

Listening is more than just hearing, and seeing is more than just having an image in your eyes. Things that come before our ears and eyes can be completely unnoticed, unless we're paying attention. God will continue to speak and reveal Truth. Take the effort to really listen.

—Sharri Larson

Prayer: Dear God, make us ready to hear your voice and see your face. Speak so that we can hear. Show us how to live. In Jesus' name, amen.

One 2 ONE

WHERE'S THE GOOD Samaritan?

> Matthew 25:40
> Luke 10:25-37

I was driving down the street on my way to church when my battery light came on. I lost power steering; and my engine started making a loud, clanking sound. The temperature gauge started to rise. I thought about trying to make it to church, but gave up when the temperature got dangerously high. I pulled into the entrance of another local church.

My first thought was, *Man, this is going to cost me.* My second thought was, *How am I going to get to church?* I had my cell phone and the church directory. I am proud to say that on my first try I found someone willing to pick me up and bring me to church.

While I was waiting, I had a strange feeling. I was sitting there in the entrance to a church, with the hood of my car raised. A car started to pull in. The driver slowed down but didn't stop. Then another car pulled through; this one didn't even slow down. Several cars drove up before one finally stopped to offer assistance.

I am reminded of the parable of the good Samaritan. How many of us would have passed by without offering help? I am sorry

to say that I probably would have too. These days, it's hard to know when it is safe to offer help.

But what about other situations. How many times do we pass by someone at school just because they look a little different? How often does someone new enter our church, and we don't even offer a smile?

Aside from taking a chunk out of my wallet, this incident has made me stop and think. I wonder if I'm doing all I can to be the person God wants me to be. Remember the Scripture "Just as you did it to one of the least of these, . . . you did to me"? What are we doing to the least of these?

—John Stevens

Prayer: Loving God, help me see the least, the lost, and the last around me. Show me how to love them like Jesus did. In Jesus' name, amen.

One 2 ONE

YOU CAN *Overcome*

> Romans 5:1-5
> Hebrews 10:36-36
> James 1:2-4 5:1-5

The drive was long—really long. It took Doug and me two and a half days to get there. Floyd (my car) was good to us. We shed mile after mile as we went west on Interstate 40. With only anticipation to combat, our trip was going as planned. As we made our way from the hill country of Tennessee and Alabama, only one thing was on our minds: the canyon. Being good Americans we were fulfilling our duty by visiting the Grand Canyon of Arizona and Utah. The adventure started months before, when we planned our trip. We wanted not only to see the great gorge, we wanted to experience it. It was finally time to go. We tossed our packs and gear in Floyd and off we went.

In case you have never been to the Grand Canyon, take my word for it: it is big, vast, huge, mammoth, gigantic—really quite large, one could say. Once we made it there, we were like two little boys at Christmas. We were excited yet nervous. We knew that we were in for something amazing as we took photos and talked about how cool it was that we were finally there and about to go into the canyon. We were awestruck by this

masterpiece that nature has been working on for as many years as words it would take to describe its beauty.

Early that next day we donned our packs, grabbed our Gatorade® and headed for Horseshoe Mesa. We went down as boys, and came up as men. At least, that's how we felt.

God had many lessons for us to learn on our trip to the Grand Canyon. One big one was the lesson of endurance. Doug and I were not experienced hikers. And we did very little to get ourselves physically ready for the undertaking. The terrain was tough. One wrong step could mean trouble and a one-way trip to the bottom—the fast way. Going up was slow and as treacherous as coming down. One mile per hour was our rate of travel.

We were in way over our heads, and we knew it. It was going to take everything we had and more to make it to the top. We also knew that using God's strength could get us out of any mess we got ourselves into. That land was obviously filled with God's glorious creative love; we relied on that love for inner-strength.

Doug and I made it to the top eventually. We paced ourselves, took our time, took care of each other, and never took our eyes off our goal. God's love gave us what we needed to make it through our journey.

In your daily life, you may find yourself over your head as we did. At school, you may have given into negative peer pressure, your parents may heap a mountain of high expectations on you, you and your best friend may be going through a tough time, or work may be hard to find. Don't give up; take strength from God. Persevere. Don't take your eyes off your goal, but rather keep them fixed on Jesus. Don't spend time dwelling on the problems in life, look for solutions.

If you and your friends are having trouble, take care of each other. If the peer pressure is too much, reach out to friends and family to help you carry the load. Jesus is there for you. He didn't give up on his disciples, and he won't give up on you. He endured the cross and can help you get through your trials. As you hike your trails, be sure to take a friend, take care of each other, pace the trip, and use God's love to give you strength. God will not give you more than you can handle.

—Paul Harcey

Prayer: God, the road is long; but thanks to you, we are not alone. You give us guidance. You give us companions. Most of all, you walk with us. Thank you for your presence. In Jesus' name, amen.

One 2 ONE

Theme Index

One 2 ONE

Scripture Index